the
**WEEKEND
CRAFTER**

MACRAME

2

the WEEKEND CRAFTER

MACRAME

19 GREAT WEEKEND PROJECTS

LARK
CRAFTS

An Imprint of
Sterling Publishing Co., Inc.
New York

WWW.LARKCRAFTS.COM.

EDITOR:
TERRY TAYLOR

ART DIRECTOR & PRODUCTION:
SUSAN MCBRIDE
TOM METCALF

PHOTOGRAPHY:
EVAN BRACKEN

ILLUSTRATIONS:
ORRIN LUNDGREN

EDITORIAL ASSISTANT:
RAIN NEWCOMB

PRODUCTION ASSISTANCE:
HANNES CHAREN
SHANNON YOKELEY

Library of Congress Cataloging-in-Publication Data

Gentry, Jim.
Macrame: 19 great weekend projects to make / Jim Gentry.
        p. cm. – (The weekend crafter)
Includes index.
ISBN 978-1-4547-0180-4 (pb. : alk. paper)
1. Macrame. I. Title. II. Series.
TT879.B3C73 2011
746.41'2—dc21
                                2003002787
10 9 8 7 6 5 4 3 2 1

Published by Lark Crafts, An Imprint of
Sterling Publishing Co., Inc.
387 Park Avenue South, New York, NY 10016

First published in 2002 by Lark Books, A Division of Sterling Publishing Co., Inc.

Previously published as Macrame: 20 Great Projects to Knot

© 2011 Lark Crafts, An Imprint of Sterling Publishing Co., Inc.
Text © 2002, BJ Crawford

Distributed in Canada by Sterling Publishing
c/o Canadian Manda Group, 165 Dufferin Street
Toronto, Ontario, Canada M6K 3H6

Distributed in the United Kingdom by GMC Distribution Services,
Caste Place, 166 High Street, Lewes, East Sussex, England BN7 1XU

Distributed in Australia by Capricorn Link (Australia) Pty Ltd.,
P.O. Box 704, Windsor, NSW 2756 Australia

The written instructions, photographs, designs, patterns, and projects in this volume are intended for the personal use of the reader and may be reproduced for that purpose only. Any other use, especially commercial use, is forbidden under law without written permission of the copyright holder.

Every effort has been made to ensure that all the information in this book is accurate. However, due to differing conditions, tools, and individual skills, the publisher cannot be responsible for any injuries, losses, and other damages that may result from the use of the information in this book.

If you have questions or comments about this book, please contact:
Lark Crafts
67 Broadway
Asheville, NC 28801
828-253-0467

Manufactured in China

ISBN 13: 978-157990-280-3 (original edition) 978-1-4547-0180-4 (current edition)

For information about custom editions, special sales, premium and corporate purchases, please contact Sterling Special Sales Department at 800-805-5489 or specialsales@sterlingpub.com.

For information about desk and examination copies available to college and university professors, requests must be submitted to academic@larkbooks.com. Our complete policy can be found at www.larkcrafts.com.

CONTENTS

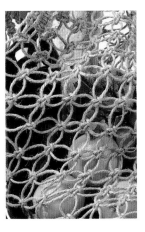

INTRODUCTION

Knots and knotting! Macrame! Why knot? Well, we always have. We teach our children to tie their shoes, anchor our tents on overnight camping trips, tie our dinghies to the dock, and lovingly tie fanciful ribbon bows on gift packages. We use knots every day, though today we're more likely to use a wire core twist-tie or an elastic bungee cord instead of knotted cord. The act of knotting—whether practical or artistic—has an appeal that, once discovered, can become a lifelong pursuit.

Knotting as a practical skill is likely as old as man. Vines, stripped barks, grasses, and animal sinew were used in a variety of ways in early cultures. Using knotting for adornment defined early cultures, and reflected the development of intelligence and the complex structure of the culture.

Historic artifacts illustrate man's creative effort through the ages. Elaborately knotted military regalia in both European and Asian cultures, reflected an interest in creating beauty and symbolizing power through texture, pattern, and color. We find major examples of the creative use of knotting (as a popular form of women's needlework) in the Victorian era due to the increased varieties of ready-made materials and the rise of leisure time. Seafaring men on board sailing ships in the nineteenth century used the materials at hand (and the idle hours of life at sea) to knot complex works for loved ones at home.

As a young boy growing up on a farm I remember large hanks of golden-colored sisal string hanging in the barn. The string had a practical use: it held together har-vested bales of hay. When the strings were removed from the bales—in order to feed the livestock—the sisal was saved for future use. It was secured in an orderly fashion to a wooden beam with a lark's head knot (though I didn't know what the knot was called at the time). I used this abundant supply of sisal to pull toys, secure firewood to a small red wagon, and to create a precarious barn loft swing secured with simple overhand knots. It was a fiber that I was intimately familiar with in all its uses.

In graduate school, I had the good fortune to have studied with professors who allowed me to explore the uses of fiber beyond those of the weaving studio. The art of macrame was undergoing a revival in the twentieth century. It was everywhere: in craft books, art exhibitions, and items of popular culture. I was roped in by knotting, so to speak.

On a leave of absence from teaching art in the public school system, a visual arts residency provided me with the opportunity to pursue knotting creatively on a full-time basis. I designed and sold knotted projects, both simple and complex. Belts, bands, neckpieces, bags, and sculptural forms were created using the inherent qualities of fiber and how it may be shaped through knotting.

Why knot, you ask? The answer is simple. Knotting materials appeal to the senses. The textures delight our sense of touch and the colors seduce the eye. The act of knotting is portable and requires few tools, if any, aside from the human hand. In a world of mass produced goods, the act of creating objects with simple materials—for practical use or artistic pleasure —has not lost its appeal. That's why knot.

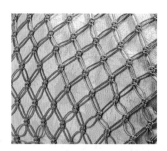

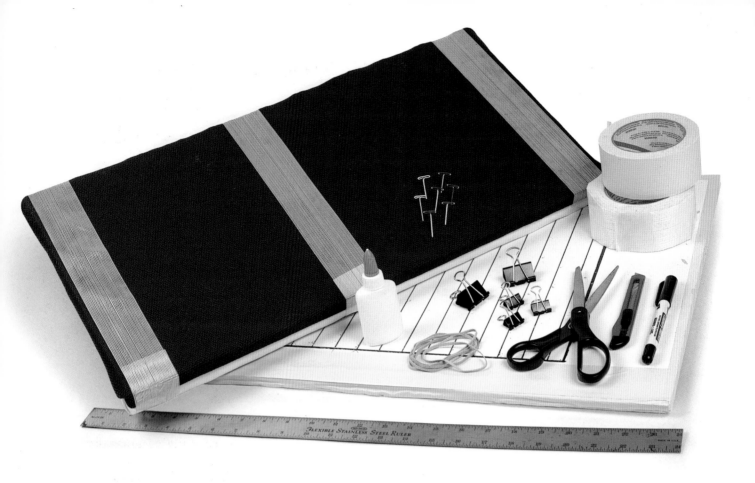

Macrame Basics

Knotting materials, a cutting tool, a knotting board, and your hands are basically all you need to create a project with macrame. Any additional tools you might need for specific projects are inexpensive and easy to acquire. In fact, you probably have many of them on hand already: scissors, a ruler or tape measure, masking or duct tape, sewing needles, a box cutter or craft knife, T-pins, paper clamps, and clear-drying waterproof glue.

CREATING A KNOTTING BOARD

A covered fiber board is an essential working surface for most macrame projects. It's a portable and flat surface tnat's easy to work on. In addition, you can easily pin cords to its porous surface. A single-layer board covered with fabric will work for many projects. If you can see several macrame projects in your future, you may want to create a more versatile two-panel board, covered with contrasting fabrics (black and white are good choices). The double thickness of the board makes it sturdier, and you can work on the side that provides the best contrast for the cords in your project.

YOU WILL NEED

Fiberboard ceiling panel (a panel for modular ceilings), measuring 24 x 48 inches (61 x 122 cm)*

2 lengths of fabric in contrasting colors, each measuring approximately 16 x 24 inches (40.6 x 60.9 cm)

Ruler

Craft knife or box cutter

Stapler and staples

Sturdy tape (fiber–reinforced strapping tape, duct tape, or masking tape), at least 2 inches (5 cm) wide

* You'll find this panel at most home improvement stores in the ceiling tile section.

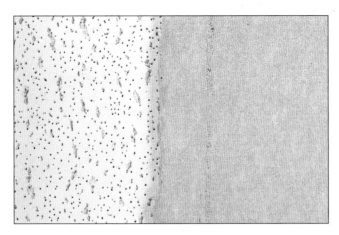

1 Examine your panel. You'll see that it has two different-looking sides. This is important. You'll want to work on the less porous side when you knot; it's smoother and will hold pins better than the rough-textured side.

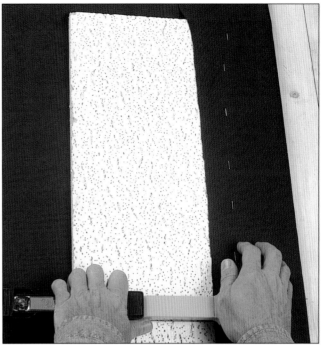

3 Spread one length of fabric on a flat, smooth work surface. Center a panel—smooth side down—on one color of fabric. Fold one long fabric edge onto the back of the fiber board. Staple the edge of the fabric to the board. Cover the raw edge of the fabric with a long strip of duct or masking tape if desired. Pull on the opposite edge of fabric to tighten the fabric on the front. Staple the fabric to the board. Tape the edge if you wish. Repeat this process with the fabric edges at each end. Create a second panel in the same way using the second color of fabric.

2 Measure and mark your panel to create two rectangles. Each rectangle should measure 12 x 18 inches (30.5 x 45.7 cm). Cut the panel with a craft knife or box cutter.

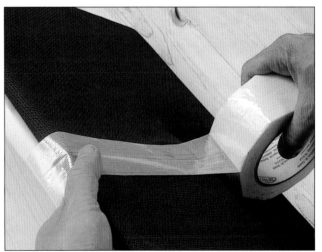

4 Hold the two fabric-covered panels back to back. Wrap a strip of tape around the center of both boards. Then wrap tape at each end around the boards.

KNOTTING MATERIALS

There's a vast array of knotting materials in an almost limitless palette of colors and size, available in craft stores, needlework shops, discount stores, and even home improvement centers. A choice between synthetic versus natural materials is a personal choice or may be dictated by the specific project.

Rayon, nylon, polypropylene, and even plastic, are favored synthetic fibers, to name just a few. Cotton, wool, silk, linen, sisal, and blends are readily available in a wide range of colors and textures. But don't limit yourself to what you would normally define as fiber. Soft, pliable, and brightly-colored wire can be found in craft stores. Precious metal wires in silver and gold are available for the truly adventurous knotter.

When you choose threads or cords for a project keep in mind how the piece is going to be used. Soft fibers like wool and silk may lose knotting definition, and may not be very strong. The lovely and soft turquoise-colored wool you covet may not be the most practical choice for a sturdy shopping bag. Instead, look for a brightly colored sisal or nylon. A beaded, silk pet leash might appeal to Fifi's sense of style, but a more durable, waterproof nylon cord is a better choice. But why make a hatband with rugged leather lacing if you have your heart set on silk? A silk hatband won't receive much wear and tear, so choose what your heart desires.

In short: choose a sturdy fiber if you expect lots of wear and tear; choose what you will if you foresee a gentle life ahead for the project.

It's essential to note that the smaller the cord, the greater the challenge of the project. That doesn't mean it can't be done; it just means it may not be as easy as it looks to use very small cords for knotting. It's a good idea to practice tying basic knots with a large, braided cord (especially if you've not knotted before!). It's an exercise that pays big dividends on future projects. Even if you've knotted before, using large cord to reacquaint yourself with the knots used in a project is a good idea.

EMBELLISHMENTS AND HARDWARE

Beads are frequently an integral part of many designs. They're readily available in a bewildering array of sizes, shapes, and materials. It's always a good idea to purchase the knotting material for your project before you choose beads and findings. Though you can enlarge the holes in beads to some extent, it's easier to find beads that you like to fit the threads you're using in a project. Read through the knotting directions to determine how many strands need to fit through a bead, then take a sample of your strands to the bead store. Following this simple hint will make your project a pleasure, rather than a trial, to work on.

O-rings and swivel snap-hooks are useful for anchoring cords for projects, such as the water bottle tote (page 58) and the pet leash (page 26). Wooden or bamboo rings, twigs or dowels, also may be used for anchor bars. But don't limit yourself! It's great fun to use found objects or unexpected anchors in your knotting designs.

KNOTTING TERMS AND DEFINITIONS

Macrame, like knitting, crochet, tatting, and weaving, is a system of creating a fiber structure. Unlike other methods, which depend upon looping or threads running over and under each other, macrame creates a structure with secured knots. That is, tying knots with selected cords, regrouping cords as needed and tying more knots.

A thread is a cord is a strand is a...

Threads, cords, strands, ropes. They all mean the same in macrame instructions: a length of fiber. Writers like to use different terms to pep up their prose. In one project instruction you may be told to regroup the strands and tie double-half hitches with the cords. Knot with what you have!

Abbreviations

You'll find abbreviations in every set of instructions for crochet, knitting, and other fiber projects. These abbreviations make reading the instructions easier and less repetitive. In the instructions for the projects in this book you may read "tie a row of reverse double half hitches (RDHHs)." The next time this knot is used in the instructions you will read "tie a row of RDHHs." Abbreviations save time and valuable space.

Active and Inactive Threads

Active threads are being moved: tying the knots. *Inactive* threads are not being used to tie knots. In macrame, threads are continually changing functions; inactive threads may become active threads in the next steps of a design. If the directions tell you "to make these threads inactive", it literally means to not use the threads in that step.

Alternating and Regrouping

For most projects, cords will be separated into and worked in groups. A group of four is most commonly used, but groups of two, three, or any number may be used. Most, but not all, designs are created using a total number of cords divisible by four.

Regrouping cords is simply a process of joining a specified number of cords from two adjacent groups. Each project will describe how cords are to be regrouped in each step as needed.

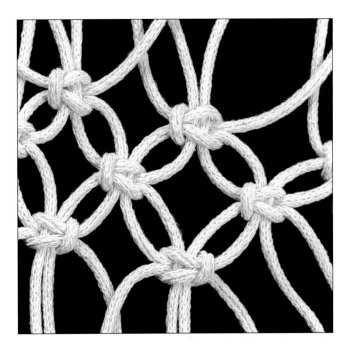

The word *alternating* is frequently used in macrame design language. For example: "Tie five rows of alternating square knots, using 16 total strands." This means that the first row will have four single square knots. You will regroup the cords and tie a second row of three square knots. Cords at each end of the row will be inactive. Regroup again, and tie a row of square knots.

The place mat (page 24) and shopping bag (page 62) use an alternating structure as an integral part of their designs.

Anchoring Cords

In order to tie cords they must be taut, or offer some resistance to the act of tying. This is accomplished by attaching or anchoring the cords in some fashion. It also helps to keep the threads in order. Each project will specify how the cords should be mounted.

A *slip-loop knot* (page 15) is used when threads are small and may be hard to identify as separate strands. This knot is easy to remove: you simply pull one end of the loop and the knot is removed. The slip-loop knot is a variation of the overhand knot.

The *overhand knot* (page 14) is used when cords are heavy and individual strands are easy to see. If you're working from one end, the knot may remain for the duration of the work; it may be removed at any point after the work is underway; or it may be an integral part of the design. In projects worked from the midpoint, the knot must be removed before completing the design in the opposite direction.

A *lark's head knot* (page 14) is used when there is a fixed anchor for the knotting cords. An O-ring, buckle, snap-hook, or separate length of cord are all fixed anchors. These fixed anchors are usually an integral part of the project design.

Cord Length (and how to handle it)

Generally if cords are no longer than 3 yards (2.7 m), they will be fairly easy to work with, and time will be saved by leaving them loose. The key to working with long cords is to have an uncluttered and clear, open work area. In addition, when each knot is begun, keep the loop open for the cord you are pulling through to form the knot.

Some knotters wind long cords into bundles which are often referred to as "butterflies." The bundles may be secured with rubber bands, tied with a short cord, or held with paper clamps. But other knotters find this method cumbersome. As you work, you will discover which you prefer—using bundles, or leaving the cords free.

Dimensions of Finished Projects

Remember that all dimensions for finished projects are approximate. The dimensions are based on the specific materials used and how tightly (or loosely) the project is knotted. No two knotters knot with the same tension. But don't worry, the cord lengths in each project are sized generously to compensate for this effect.

Knotting and Knot-Bearing Strands

Cords have two primary functions in macrame: *knotting* or *knot-bearing*. A knot-bearing strand is usually held taut, and the knotting strand is moved around the taut strand. It should be noted that cords change functions. A knot-bearing strand in one step may become a knotting strand in the next step.

Level of Difficulty

What makes one project more difficult than another? Four different elements determine the level of difficulty for a specific project. These elements are: the size of thread used, the number of knots used, the number of design changes in the project, and the scale of the project.

The projects in this book are divided into three levels of difficulty: easy, somewhat difficult, and moder-

ately difficult. Start with an easy project if macrame is a new craft for you. The projects you'll find on pages 20 through 38 are designed for beginners. If you're an old hand at macrame or have knotted some of the easy projects in this book, you'll find more challenging projects on pages 41 through 62. The last three projects in the book are moderately difficult.

Sinnet

A *sinnet* of square knots results from two or more knots being tied with the same four cords. If the instructions are to tie a sinnet of 17 square knots, don't panic. Tie 17 square knots.

Working Methods

Different projects require different working methods. The working method to use is determined by the design of the project itself. There are three working methods used to create the projects in this book.

Knotting in the round is creating a continuous structure with no edges. It results when the knotting cords are anchored continuously around an object or holding form. The eyeglass case (page 47), key ring pouch (page 51), and shopping bag are examples of knotting in the round. All are worked from the top down, then closed (tied off) at the bottom of the design.

Knotting from one end is simply working from one end to the opposite end. It's used when the strands needed to complete the project are relatively short or when the project must be anchored at one end. The watchband (page 54) and the water bottle tote (page 58) are good examples of this working method.

Knotting from the midpoint is working from the center or midpoint of a design. It's useful when working with very long cords. The working length of the cords is divided in half (usually with an overhand knot). You work the design as directed, turn the knotting board, and work the design again. The place mat (page 24) and the hatband (page 36) are both examples of this method of working.

BASIC KNOTS

You've read about knots and how to use them. Now, let's look at a knot as if you've never seen one before. Knots are known by different (and sometimes colorful) names. In this section you'll find a photograph and an illustration for each knot you'll use for projects in this book. More importantly, you'll learn how each one is tied! Refer to this section often if you're a novice knotter.

Square Knot (SQKT)

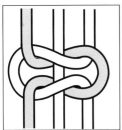

The square knot is a secure, non-slipping knot made over a central core or knot-bearing strand of one or more threads. The knot-bearing strand should be kept taut when you make this knot. Practice this knot. Practice it again and again. You'll soon develop a personal method for holding the core cords taut.

Pass the right-hand cord over the core cords and under the left-hand cord, leaving a little loop on the right. Then pass the left-hand cord under the core cords and up through the loop. Pull the cords to tighten the first half of the knot.

Then pass the left-hand cord over the core cords and under the right-hand cord, leaving a little loop on the left. Now, pass the right-hand cord under the core cords and up through the loop. Pull the cords to tighten the finished knot.

Half Knot (HK)

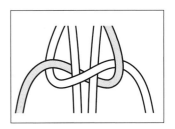

This is simply one half of the square knot. When tied repeatedly, it results in a spiral sinnet of half knots. The spiral may twist clockwise or counter-clockwise depending on which cord— the left or right—is placed over the core threads.

Half Hitch (HH)

This knot is made of a single loop over one or more knot-bearing threads. Hold the knot-bearing thread taut, loop a knotting strand around the knot-bearing strand, then pull it into place.

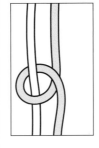

Alternating Half Hitch (AHH)

Not really a single knot, but a knot pattern, is created by alternating the thread used as the knot-bearing strand. Tie a half hitch, then switch: the knot-bearing cord now becomes the knotting cord. Then tie a half hitch. When two strands of different colors are used, a predictable and decorative pattern results.

Lark's Head Knot (LHK)

This is the knot most commonly used to anchor doubled cords. Find the midpoint of your cord and fold it in half forming a loop. Bring the looped end of the cord under the anchoring cord (ring, buckle, or dowel) from the top. The free ends are placed through the loop and the loop is pulled tight.

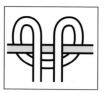  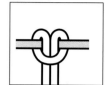

Overhand Knot (OK)

You use this basic knot almost daily without thinking about it. Try tying your shoes without it. It's used to anchor cords at the beginning of projects , as well as a finishing knot. Make a loop. Bring the end of the cord behind the loop and out through the loop. Pull it tight.

Slip-Loop Knot (SLK)

This a variation of the overhand knot. It's tied by creating a loop around two fingers. Then reach through the loop and pull the free strand or strands through the loop forming a second loop. Pull it snugly, but keep an open loop as you create a knot below.

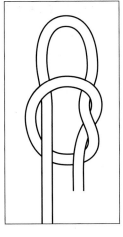

Double Half Hitch (DHH)

Double-half hitches and square knots are the most frequently used knots in macrame. When a series of knotting strands are used to tie double half hitches on the same knot-bearing strand, a ridged row or line results.

Tie a half hitch around a taut knot-bearing cord. Tie another half hitch with the same knotting strand around the cord. Pick up the next free knotting strand and repeat. It's really that simple.

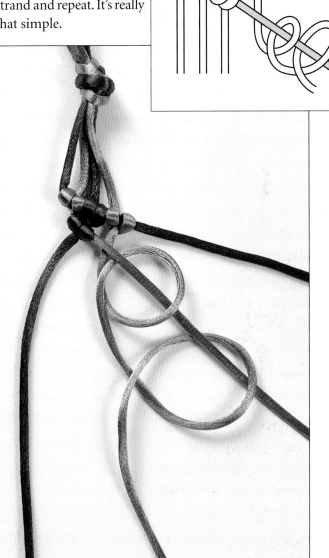

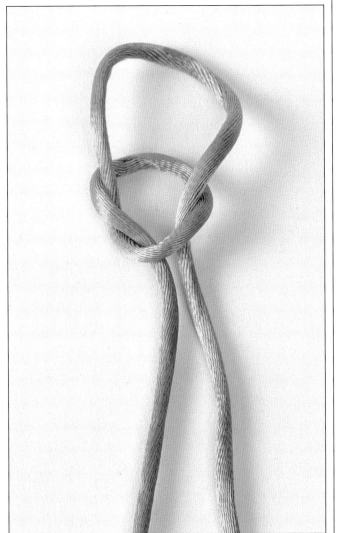

Reverse Double Half Hitch (RDHH)

This is a versatile knot that has the look of the lark's head knot turned to the side. The first step of the reverse double-half hitch is a simple half hitch. The second step is slightly different. Pass the knotting strand under and around the knot-bearing strand, and down through the loop created. It sounds simple, but here's the hitch (so to speak):

When you knot on the right side of a design, the knot-bearing strand should be held with the left hand, and the knotting strand held with the right hand.

When working on the left side of the design, hold the knot-bearing strand with the right hand and the knotting strand with the left.

It will feel awkward at first, but with practice it becomes comfortable and ensures a consistent knot pattern.

Coil Knot (CK)

This is similar to an overhand knot. It adds a decorative accent to the loose ends of strands, and it keeps strands from unraveling.

Make a large overhand knot. Before you close that knot, take one cord end and wrap it four times (or more) around the looped strand, then pull the knot firmly into place.

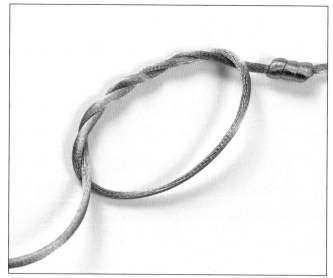

Gathering Double Half Hitch (GDHH)

Use this knot when you need to bring together a number of cords spread across a design.

Tie double half hitches in the usual way. However, instead of placing knotting strands aside after they are used, combine them with the knot-bearing cord just used. The process continues across the design until all strands are gathered in a bundle at the end of the knotted row.

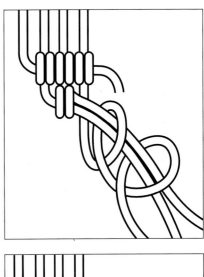

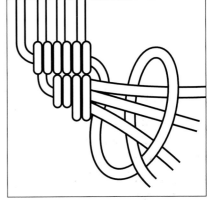

Three-Ply Braid

This simplest of braids is created using three strands or three groups of multiple threads. A braid works well in many knotted designs as a transition from one pattern to the next. And it works up quickly!

You have strands on the left, center, and right. Pick up the left strand and place it over the center strand. Then pick up the right strand and place it over the center strand. The sequence does not vary: left over center, right over center. If the sequence is interrupted, you'll see your mistake at once.

Four-Ply Braid

Yes, it's slightly more complicated than the three-ply braid. It creates a rounded rather than a flat braid. When you use more than one color, lovely patterns appear in the braid. Practice this braid and then practice it again.

Maintain constant tension on all the strands as you braid. Pick up the left strand. Bring it behind the next two strands and back in between those two strands. Pick up the right strand. Bring it behind the adjacent two strands and back in-between the two. Repeat this sequence until you have the desired length.

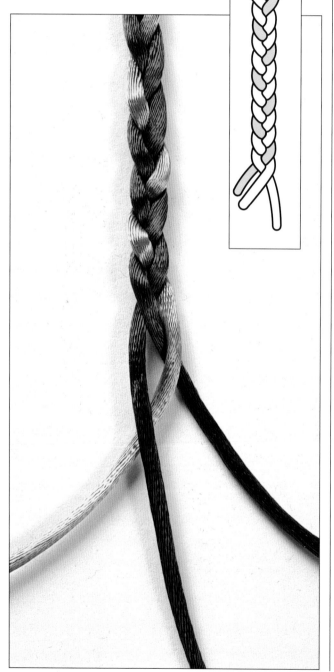

QUICK KNOT REFERENCE

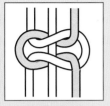

SQUARE KNOT
(SQKT)

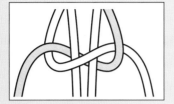

HALF KNOT
(HK)

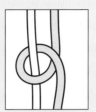

HALF HITCH
(HH)

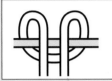 

LARK'S HEAD KNOT (LHK)

ALTERNATING
HALF HITCH(AHH)

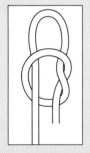

SLIP-LOOP KNOT
(SLK)

DOUBLE HALF HITCH (DHH)

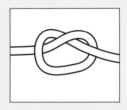

OVERHAND KNOT
(OHK)

REVERSE DOUBLE
HALF HITCH (RDHH)

COIL KNOT
(CK)

THREE-PLY
BRAID

FOUR-PLY BRAID

GATHERING DOUBLE HALF HITCH (GDHH)

Snug-as-a-Bug Mug Rugs

Tie up these thirsty coasters to protect your table from the heat of winter's mug of hot chocolate or from the moisture of a summery tumbler of gin and tonic. They're quick and extremely easy to knot. Make a set of them to match the place mats on page 24 or several sets to use as gifts.

YOU WILL NEED

176 feet (53.7 m) of braided cotton cord ⅛ inch (3 mm) in diameter (for 4 coasters)

Ruler or tape measure

Scissors

Knotting board

T-pins

DIMENSIONS OF FINISHED PIECE
3 x 5 inches (7.6 x 12.7 cm)

KNOTS AND WORKING METHOD
Overhand knot (OK), square knot (SQKT)

Knotting from one end

Preparing the Materials

For each coaster, cut 20 pieces of cord, each one measuring 26 inches (66 cm) long.

1   Tie a set of four cords with an OK about 3 inches (7.6 cm) from the end. Make five sets in all.

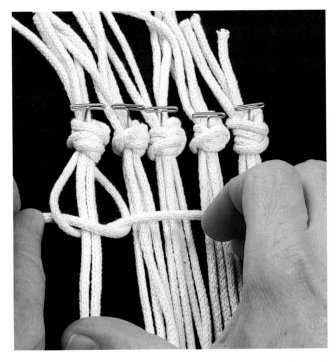

2   Anchor the five sets of cords to the knotting board side-by-side, with a T-pin through each OK. Tie one SQKT in each group of four threads. Make sure the knots line up side-by-side.

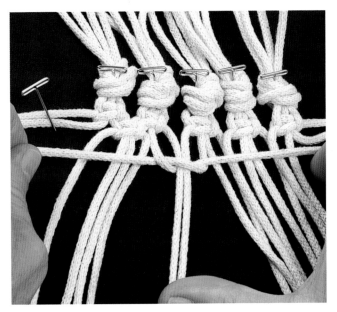

3   Start at the left. Place two cords to the side; they are now inactive. Make a SQKT using the next four threads. Make a row of square knots, leaving two inactive at the end of the row. Knot a total of 13 rows of alternating square knots. Pull the ends of the last row of knots securely. Trim the cord ends with scissors as desired.

4   Remove the t-pins and untie the overhand knots. Pull the ends tightly and trim the cord ends.

Soft Suede Belt

Oh, so retro...but chic and simple. A suede belt will complement casual wear, so why not knot a silk cord belt for dressy evening wear?

DIMENSIONS
OF FINISHED PIECE

26 inches (66 cm) long, not including tying strands

YOU WILL NEED

24 feet (7.3 m) of brown suede lacing, approximately ⅛ inch (3 mm) wide

16 feet (4.9 m) of tan suede lacing, approximately ⅛ inch (3 mm) wide

Tape measure or ruler

Scissors

T-pins

Knotting board

KNOTS AND WORKING METHOD

Overhand knot (OK), square knot (SQKT)

Knotting from the midpoint

Preparing the Materials

Determine what size belt you want to make. For a longer belt, add length to the knotting strands in a 5-to-1 ratio. For example, if you need to add 6 inches (15.2 cm) to the length, add 30 inches to each strand you need.

Cut three pieces of brown lacing, each measuring 8 feet (2.4 m) long or to your measurement. Cut two pieces of tan leather lacing to the same measurement. Hold the five suede strands together, identify the midpoint, and tie an overhand knot using all five strands.

1 Use a T-pin to anchor the OK to the knotting board. Arrange the strands: tan on the outside, three brown in the middle. Pick up the tan cord on the left, combine with two brown to the right, and tie one SQKT using one knot-bearing cord. Lay the tan lace to the side. Tie one SQKT with three brown cords. Pull the knot up to and just below the first knot you tied.

2 Pick up the tan cord on the right, combine it with two brown cords, and tie one SQKT. Tie one SQKT with three brown cords. Pull the knot up to and just below the first knot you tied.

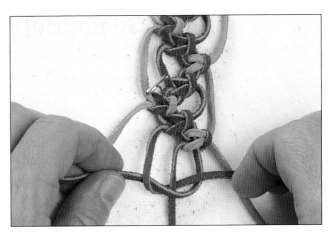

3 Repeat steps 1 and 2 six times. You've completed almost half of the belt.

4 Use the tan laces as knotting strands. Tie three SQKTs around the brown laces. Pull the last knot snugly. Remove the T-pin from the OK and untie the knot. Anchor the belt to the board. Knot the second half of the belt as described in steps 1, 2, and 3. Repeat the design sequence of four knots a total of nine times.

5 Finish the ends of the leather cords with coil knots. Vary the position of the coil knots, if you wish to create different lengths for the cord ends.

Dinner for Two (Three or Four) Place Mat

This is a great introductory project for the novice knotter. The cords (and knots) are large and easy to manage. You'll be surprised just how quickly the project can be finished. Go ahead: knot a pair for tonight's dinner while the chicken is roasting in the oven.

DIMENSIONS
OF FINISHED PIECE
12 x 21 inches (30.5 x 53.3 cm) including the fringe

YOU WILL NEED
85 yards (77.7 m) of braided cotton cord (per mat)
Ruler or tape measure
Scissors
T-pins
Knotting board marked with a 1-inch (2.5 cm) grid.*

*If you don't wish to mark a grid on your fabric-covered knotting board, mark the grid on a piece of paper the same size as your board. Pin or tape the paper to the board.

KNOTS AND WORKING METHOD
Square knot (SQKT), overhand knot (OK)

Knotting from the midpoint

Preparing the Materials

For each place mat, measure and cut 36 pieces of cotton cord, each 7 feet (2.1 m) long. Gather four strands at a time. Tie an overhand knot (OK) in each group at the midpoint. Repeat until you have nine groups.

1 Mark your knotting board with a 12 x 19-inch (30.5 x 48.3 cm) grid of 1-inch (2.5 cm) squares. This grid will help you keep the knots evenly spaced.

2 Anchor each group of cords to the mid-line of your grid with a T-pin through the OK.

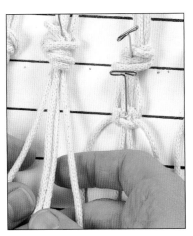

3 Tie one SQKT in each group. Pull the first half of the knot up to the line. Pin it in place. Finish the second half of the knot, pulling it securely. Continue tying and pinning one SQKT in each of the nine groups.

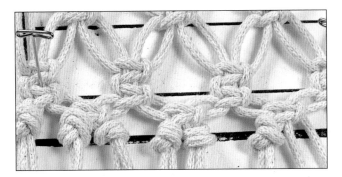

4 Regroup the cords for the next row. Leave two threads inactive on the left side. Use the next four threads to tie one SQKT. Tie one SQKT in each regrouped group of four across the row. On the right side you will end with two inactive threads. Regroup the cords again. Knot a total of eight rows of alternating square knots. As the work progresses, move the T-pins down to secure the next knotted row.

5 Knot a ninth row with two SQKTs in each group. Regroup and knot a 10th row with one SQKT in each group, pulling it up closely to the previous row. Starting on the left, tie an overhand knot with two cords together. Pull the knot snugly. Repeat across the row, finishing this half of the mat. Trim the ends evenly.

6 Reverse the position of the knotting board. Remove the OKs. Knot the second half of the place mat with seven alternating rows of SQKTs. Rows eight and nine should be knotted and finished as described in step 5.

Red Rover Pet Leash

"Red Rover, Red Rover, send…" Fido (or Floyd or Spot!) right over into canine chic with this sturdy leash.

DIMENSIONS
OF FINISHED PIECE

60 inches (1.5 m) from hand-hold to swivel snap-hook

YOU WILL NEED

20 yards (18.2 m) of small twisted nylon cord, approximately ⅛ inch (3 mm) in diameter

Swivel snap-hook (available at hardware and home supply stores)

Ruler or measuring tape

Scissors

Knotting board

T-pins

Clear-drying white craft glue

KNOTS AND WORKING METHOD

Lark's head knot (LHK), overhand knot (OK), square knot (SQKT)

Knotting from one end

Preparing the Materials

Measure and cut two pieces of cord each 28 feet (8.5 m) long. Fold each cord in half at the midpoint. Mount each doubled cord on the swivel hook with a LHK.

1 Use the two inside cords as knot-bearing cords and the outer cords as knotting cords. Tie four SQKTs. Exchange the outside knotting cords with the inside knot-bearing cords.

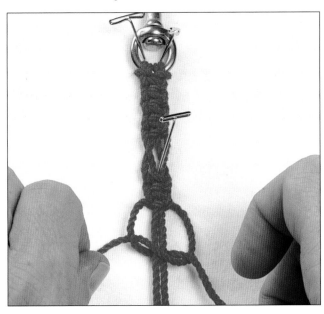

2 Create an opening 1 inch (2.54 cm) below the last SQKT. Position a T-pin in the board, below the four knots, to hold the space. Tie four SQKT with the cords in the new positions. Repeat the pattern of tying four SQKT, exchanging the cords and leaving a space, and tying four more SQKT until the sinnet measures 48 inches in length.

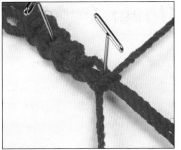

3 Exchange the position of the outside and inside strands, but leave only a ½-inch (1.3 cm) opening. With the new cord arrangement, tie 36 SQKTs.

4 Insert the two outside knotting strands in the ½-inch (1.3 cm) opening and pull them through. The 36 square knots have formed the hand-loop. Place the longer knot-bearing strands at each side of the leash body.

5 Tie two SQKTs around the entire leash body and the free strands you pulled through earlier.

6 Tie one OK in each pair of two loose strands, and pull firmly into place against the leash. Trim the cord ends close to the OK. Coat the knot with clear-drying white craft glue to prevent fraying. Allow the glue to dry before you take Fido for a walk.

Quartet of Beaded Napkin Rings

These napkin rings are a such a breeze to make that you can make several sets in different colors for yourself or as quick gifts. If hemp is not your cup of tea, use a similarly sized cord for a different look.

YOU WILL NEED

22 yards (20.1 m) of hemp, or a similar natural-colored cord, approximately ⅛ inch (3 mm) in diameter (will make a set of 4)

4 glass beads *

Knotting board

T-pins

Scissors

Clear-drying white craft glue

Cardboard tube

*Remember to take your knotting material with you when you purchase your beads. You'll thread one bead onto two strands in this project.

DIMENSIONS OF FINISHED PIECE

1½ (3.8 cm) inches in diameter

KNOTS AND WORKING METHOD

Overhand knot (OK), square knot (SQKT), double half hitch (DHH)

Knotting from one end

Preparing the Materials

Cut six lengths of cord, each 32 inches (81.2 cm) long for each napkin ring.

1 Tie an OK in a group of six strands about two inches (5 cm) from one end. Anchor the cords to your knotting board through the knot.

2 Divide the six strands into two groups of three. First row: Tie one SQKT using one group of three strands. Tie one SQKT in the second group of three strands.

Second row: Make a group of four. One cord will be inactive on either side. Tie one SQKT with the grouped cords.

Repeat these two rows of knotting three times.

3 You are now ready to tie two diagonal rows of DHHs. Think of the design in two parts: three cords on the left, and three cords on the right. Begin on either side.

Hold the outside cord across the two remaining cords and tie one row of DHHs. Pick up the outside cord again and tie a row of DHHs. Pull this row tightly against the first. Complete the design by tying two rows of DHHs on the opposite side.

Thread the two middle strands of cord through the bead and pull into place against the DHH row.

5 Remove the knotting from the board. Untie the OK and turn the knotting over. Smooth the cords, making sure that the cords are in order. Shape the work into a loose ring. Knot the cord ends in order with a square knot—just like you would to tie a package. There are no knot-bearing cords. Pull the knots evenly and securely. Tie six SQKTs in all.

4 Divide the two cords on which you threaded the bead. Pass one over the two strands to the left and one over the two strands to the right. Working from the center out, tie two rows of DHH to mirror the pattern of the DHH in step 3.

   Pick up the four strands in the middle (there will be one inactive cord on each side) and tie one SQKT. Regroup the cords into two groups of three and tie one SQKT in each group. Repeat these two rows three times to mirror the square knot pattern in step 2.

6 Slip the knotted ring onto a cardboard tube. Trim the cord ends ⅛ inches (3 mm) from each knot. Squeeze a bit of white craft glue on each SQKT. Allow the glue to dry.

True Blue Trio of Bookmarks

A trio of very different looking bookmarks has a dark (but not too deep) secret. Using only two colors of thread you can knot three very different looking bookmarks. What's the secret? We're knot telling yet. This project is a great practice piece for some tricky (and not so tricky) knots.

**DIMENSIONS
OF FINISHED PIECE**
11 inches (27.9 cm)
including fringe

YOU WILL NEED

8 yards (7.3 m) of blue cotton
crochet thread

8 yards (7.3 m) of grey cotton
crochet thread

Ruler or measuring tape

Scissors

Knotting board

T-pins

Tapestry needle

KNOTS AND WORKING METHOD
Overhand knot (OK), double half hitch
(DHH), square knot (SQKT), reverse
double half hitch (RDHH)

Working from one end

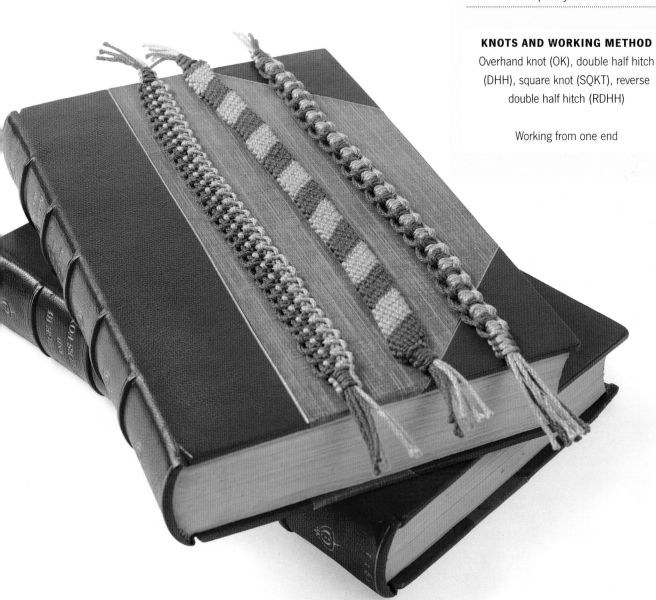

Preparing the Materials

For each bookmark, you will need eight lengths of thread, four of each color. Measure and cut each thread 4 feet (12.2 m) long. Gather eight threads together with an OK tied 4 inches (10.2 cm) from one end. Anchor the eight strands to the knotting board through the OK.

Finishing the Bookmarks

After you have followed the directions for any of the three bookmarks, finish any bookmark by tying three SQKTs, using six strands as knot-bearing strands. Turn the bookmark over. Thread a tapestry needle with a knotting thread. Pull each knotting thread under the back of the SQKT. Trim the ends flush with the loop of the first SQKT. Trim the remaining six ends as desired. Remove the OK and repeat at the opposite end.

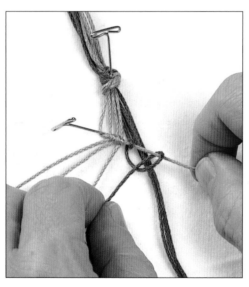

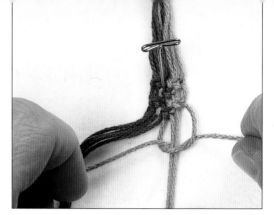

Alternating Square Knot Bookmark

2 Anchor the eight strands to the board with a T-pin through the OK. Arrange the strands into two groups: four blue on the left and four grey on the right. Tie one SQKT in each group using two strands as knot-bearing strands. Regroup the strands: two blue inactive on the left and two grey inactive on the right. Tie one SQKT with the blue and grey strands. Regroup the strands and tie two SQKTs. Repeat the alternating SQKT pattern until the knotting is about 8 inches (20.3 cm) in length.

Finish the bookmark as directed.

Double Half Hitch Bookmark

1 Anchor the strands to the knotting board with a T-pin. Arrange the eight strands: four grey on the left and four blue on the right. Pick up the outside strand on the left. Hold it diagonally across seven threads. Tie a row of DHHs, using all seven threads (see photo). Pick up the next outside strand on the left. Hold it across seven threads. Tie a row of DHHs. Continue to pick up a thread from the left and tie a row of DHHs until you have a total of 48 rows.

To finish this bookmark pick up the strand on the left and tie six DHH (row 49). Tie rows 50 through 54 with DHH, decreasing the number of DHH in each row from five to one. Then finish the bookmark as directed.

Reverse Double Half Hitch Bookmark

3 Anchor eight strands to the knotting board with a T-pin through the overhand knot. Arrange the strands: four blue on the left and four grey on the right. Hold the four middle strands taut (two blue and two grey). Tie one RDHH on the left using two blue strands. Holding the four middle strands taut, tie one RDHH on the right using the two grey strands. (Review tying RDHH on page 16 if needed). Repeat this sequence until the knotting measures 8 inches (20.3 cm) in length.

Finish the bookmark as directed.

Leather Fob Key Ring

You won't be frantically patting your pockets for keys if they're attached to this handsome key ring. Dangle the end of the finely knotted fob from your pocket, and be prepared to accept compliments from admirers.

YOU WILL NEED

8 feet (2.4 m) of rust-colored coated cotton cord, approximately ¹⁄₁₆ inch (1.6 mm) in diameter

8 feet (2.4 m) of black-colored coated cotton cord, approximately ¹⁄₁₆ inch (1.6 mm) in diameter

⅝ inch (1.6 cm) metal O-ring

Split ring

Scissors

Ruler or measuring tape

Knotting board

DIMENSIONS OF FINISHED PIECE

1½ x 10 inches (3.8 x 25.4 cm) including the fringe

KNOTS AND WORKING METHOD

Lark's head knot (LHK), double half hitch (DHH), square knot (SQKT), reverse double half hitch (RDHH), alternating half hitch (AHH), overhand knot (OK), four-ply braid

Knotting from one end

Preparing the Materials

Measure and cut two pieces of rust cord, each 4 feet (1.2 m) long; cut two pieces of black cord, each four feet (1.2 m) long. Fold each cord in half. Mount the cords on the O-ring using a LHK. Mount both black cords, then mount a rust cord on either side of the black cords. Pin the ring to the knotting board.

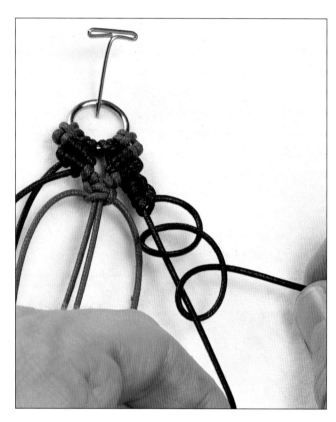

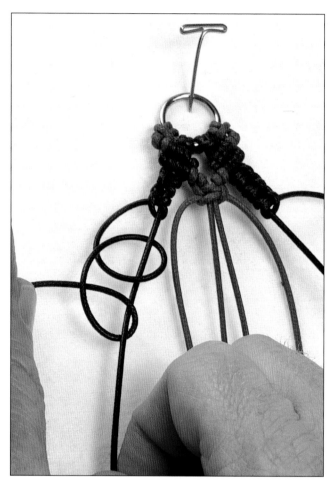

1 Pick up the outside strand on the left side. Bring it across the rust and two black strands. Tie three DHHs. Pick up the strand on the right side, hold it across the rust and two black strands toward the middle. Tie three DHHs. Pick up the rust cord on the left. Tie a second row of DHHs. Pick up the rust cord on the right. Tie a second a row of DHHs. The four rust-colored cords are now in the center. Tie a SQKT using the rust-colored cords(see photo).

2 Tie three RDHH with each set of black cords on the left and right.
Pick up one of the two rust-colored cords in the center. Use it as a knot bearing cord and tie one row of DHH working outward to the left or right. Pick up the second center cord and tie one row of DHH in the opposite direction. Tie a second row of DHH, using the rust-colored cords as knot-bearing cords, to the left and right.

3 Four black cords are now together in the center. Use two cords as knot-bearing cords. Tie four SQKTs with the four black strands. With the two rust-colored cords on the left and right, tie seven AHHs.

Divide the eight cords into groups of four (each group will contain two rust and two black cords). Tie one SQKT in each group. Regroup the cords leaving two cords on the left and right inactive. Tie one SQKT in the four cords remaining. Repeat this regrouping sequence two times.

5 Tie a second row of GDHH. See page 17 to review this knotting process.

4 Complete the design with one row of DHH worked diagonally down under the square knots.

6 Finish the key ring with a long, four-ply braid. Keep pairs of rust and black together when you braid them. When the braid is about 5 inches long (12.7 cm) long, secure it with an OK. Use scissors to trim the ends of the cords evenly or at a slight angle.

Midnight Wrangler Hatband

What urban cowboy or cowgirl wouldn't be proud to be seen two-stepping-out on a Saturday night wearing this knotted hatband on their hat?

YOU WILL NEED

32 feet (9.8 m) of fine hemp twine

20 black glass beads, approximately ⅜ inch (9.5 mm) in diameter

Scissors

Knotting board

T-pins

DIMENSIONS OF FINISHED PIECE
24 inches (61 cm) long

KNOTS AND WORKING METHOD
Overhand knot (OK), square knot (SQKT),
double half hitch (DHH)

Knotting from the midpoint

Preparing the Materials

Measure and cut six strands of twine, each 64 inches (1.6 m) long. Tie an overhand knot at the midpoint with all six strands together. Anchor the twine to the knotting board with a T-pin through the OK.

1 Tie one SQKT with four cords used as the knot-bearing cords.

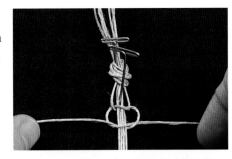

2 With the two outside cords inactive, tie two SQKT, using the four remaining strands.

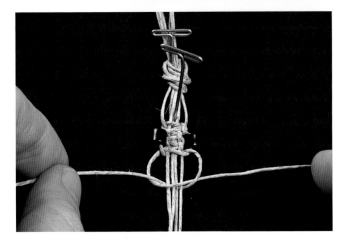

3 String one black glass bead on each of the inactive outside cords. Use these cords to tie one SQKT over four knot-bearing cords. The glass beads are held in place by the knot.

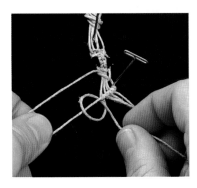

4 Anchor the outside cord on the right with a T-pin below the SQKT made in the previous step. Hold the cord diagonally across the remaining five cords. Tie one row of DHHs (see photo).

Tie one SQKT using the four cords on the right side. Tie one SQKT using the four cords on the left side. Tie one SQKT using four cords on the right side.

Anchor the outside cord on the left side with a T-pin. Hold the cord diagonally across and down over the remaining five cords. Tie a row of DHHs. This completes your first pattern.

Repeat steps 1 through 4 three times.

5 Remove the overhand knot, and anchor the knotting with a T-pin. Repeat steps 1 through 4 four times. To make the design units symmetrical you need to anchor the outside strand on the left for the first row of DHHs, working left to right. Also, you will tie the first SQKT using the four strands on the left.

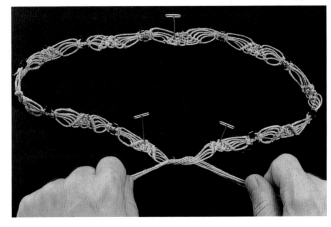

6 Wrap the knotting around the crown of the hat to estimate the needed length. Then join the two ends with a square knot. Trim the ends about 1 inch (2.5 cm) from the knot. If desired, secure the knot with a dab of clear-drying white craft glue.

Neo-Victorian Scarf Fringe

Victorian needlewomen knotted endless rows of delicate macrame edging for household articles and clothing. The simple design unit of this fringe is easy to increase for a wider scarf. If you're feeling truly Victorian, edge a tablecloth, or fringe the parlor curtains with the design.

DIMENSIONS OF FINISHED PIECE
The 6-inch (15.2 cm) fringe was designed for a 6-inch-wide (15.2 cm) scarf.*

*The simple design unit of this fringe is easy to increase for a wider scarf. Add a working unit of eight mounted cords (four blue and four green) to increase the width as needed.

KNOTS AND WORKING METHOD
Lark's head knot (LHK), square knot (SQKT), double half hitch (DHH), alternating half hitch (AHH), overhand knot (OK)

Knotting from one end

YOU WILL NEED

48 feet (14.6 m) of #3 mercerized-cotton crochet thread (navy blue)

50 feet (15.2 m) of #3 mercerized-cotton crochet thread (green)

Ruler or measuring tape

Scissors

Knotting board

T-pins

Tapestry needle

Sewing needle

Thread

Preparing the Materials

Measure and cut one piece of green thread 2 feet (60.9 cm) long. Measure and cut 32 pieces of blue and 32 pieces of green thread 3 feet (91 cm) long each. Fold the 2-foot green thread in half. Tie an OK about 2 inches (5 cm) in from each end. Pin this strand through the OKs to the knotting board. This is your anchor cord.

Find the midpoint of one blue thread. Mount the doubled thread to the anchor cord with a LHK. Mount three more blue strands, then mount four green strands. Continue mounting strands across the holding thread (four blue, four green) until all the strands are used. You will have a total of 64 knotting strands.

1 Begin knotting with the left hand group of blue strands. Tie one SQKT using two knot-bearing cords. Tie one SQKT with each group of four blue strands. You will have two blue SQKTs. Tie two SQKTs with the green strands.

Return to the previously knotted blue strands. Make two strands on the left inactive. Regroup the blue strands and tie one SQKT (see photo). Working from left to right, tie two more SQKTs. You will combine two blue strands and two green threads for one SQKT. Continue working to the right using the remaining green strands. Leave the last two green strands inactive.

Move back to the left and regroup threads for row three. Make four threads inactive. Tie a single SQKT in each group of four; leaving four threads inactive at the end of the row. You will have two knots in this row. Return to the left and regroup again. Make six threads inactive on the left. Tie one SQKT with the four remaining threads (two blue, two green). Leave six threads inactive on the right.

needle. Weave the threads of the anchor cords under the back side of the LHKs (see photo). Weave the threads approximately 1 inch (2.54 cm). Repeat on the opposite end of the anchor cord. Trim the thread ends closely with scissors.

2 Anchor the outer blue strand on the left with a t-pin. Hold the strand diagonally below the bottom of the square knots. Tie one row of DHH using the seven blue strands. Pick up the next outside blue strand and tie a second row of DHH. Repeat this sequence from the right with the green strands.

Create the long, knotted fringe with groups of two threads. Tie 40 AHHs in each group of two threads (see photo). Tie one OK below the last AHH of each two-thread unit. Work from left to right until you have created the fringe for the first design unit.

Repeat steps 1 and 2 with each of the remaining units.

4 Stitch the fringe to one end of your scarf. Make a second fringe for the opposite end of the scarf.

3 Remove the finished fringe from the board. Turn the fringe over. Untie the OK on one side, and thread the two ends of the anchor cords in the tapestry

Gossamer Pillow Overlay

Imagine coming home to one—or several—of these pillows feathering your nest. Lacy knotting adds an elegantly handcrafted touch to plain pillows.

DIMENSIONS OF FINISHED PIECE

12 x 12 inches (30.5 x 30.5 cm)

YOU WILL NEED

12-inch (30.5 cm) square pillow

132 feet (40.2 m) of nylon crochet cord

Scissors

Ruler or tape measure

Knotting board marked with a
12 x 12-inch (30.5 x 30.5 cm) grid of
1-inch (2.5 cm) squares*

T-pins

Straight pins

Sewing needle

Thread

*If you don't wish to mark a grid on your fabric-covered knotting board, mark the grid on a piece of paper the same size as your board. Pin or tape the paper to the board.

KNOTS AND WORKING METHOD

Square knot (SQKT), overhand
knot (OK)

Knotting from the midpoint

Preparing the Materials

Cut 44 pieces of cord, each three feet (.9 m) long. Gather four strands and tie an overhand knot at the midpoint of the strands. Prepare 11 groups. Anchor the overhand knots with T-pins equally spaced on the center line of the marked work board.

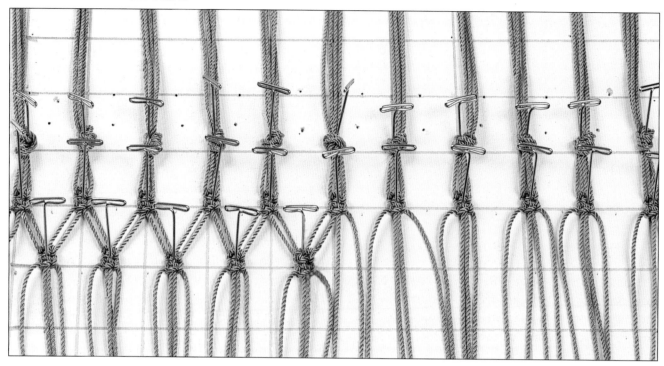

1 Tie two SQKTs in each group of four strands. Anchor each group of finished knots with a T-pin to the line on the grid. Regroup the strands into groups of four. Two strands will be inactive on the left and right. Tie two SQKT in each of the new groups of four. There will be 10 groups of square knots in this second row (see photo).

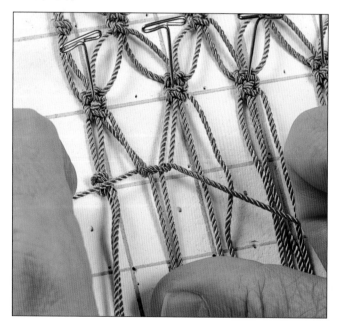

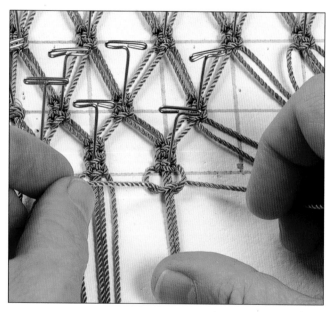

2 Tie an OK in each of the two un-knotted, inactive strands on the left and right sides. Center each OK on the grid line and secure it with a T-pin.

3 Work four more alternating rows made up of SQKTs and OKs for a total of six rows in all. Work a seventh row of SQKTs, this time with three SQKTs in each group of four.

4 Tie an OK in each group, pulled snugly against the last square knot (see photo).

Turn the board around. Remove the T-pins above from the first row of pinned OKs. Move the pins to the first row of SQKT. Untie the OKs. Follow the knotting directions in steps 1 through 3. Finish this end with Oks.

6 Thread a needle with thread to match the pillow cover. Hand stitch the knotted piece to the pillow, catching each knotted end around the outer edge of the pillow. Knots may be stitched to the cover in the center of the pillow, if desired.

5 If the pillow has a removable cover, remove the pillow. Otherwise, center the overlay on the pillow. Pin it to the pillow on all sides with straight pins.

Plum Pretty Pendant Necklace

Veteran knotters already know the pleasures of working with linen thread—it's the Rolls Royce of knotting material. This classic interpretation of a knotted necklace will introduce you to the pleasures of working with linen. But be forewarned: after finishing this piece you may never want to knot with any other fiber!

DIMENSIONS OF FINISHED PIECE

$1\frac{7}{8}$ inches (4.8 cm) at the widest point of the pendant; total necklace length is approximately 13 inches (33 cm).

YOU WILL NEED

54 feet (5.5 m) of medium-weight linen thread

$\frac{3}{8}$-inch (9.5 mm) black glass bead

12 black glass pony beads, approximately $\frac{3}{16}$ inch (5 mm) in diameter

5 frosted-glass beads, approximately $\frac{1}{4}$ inch (6 mm) in diameter

Ruler or measuring tape

Scissors

Knotting board

T-pins

KNOTS AND WORKING METHOD

Reverse double half hitch (RDHH), square knot (SQKT), slip-loop knot (SLK), double-half hitch (DHH), overhand knot (OK), three-ply braid

Knotting from one end

Preparing the Materials

Measure and cut six lengths of thread, each measuring 9 feet (2.7 m). Pick up three threads and align the cut ends. Thread all three strands through the ⅜-inch (9.5 mm) black bead. Slide the bead to the midpoint of the three strands. Set this group aside. Locate the midpoint of the three remaining strands. Tie a SLK about 4 inches (10.2 cm) above the midpoint of the remaining three strands.

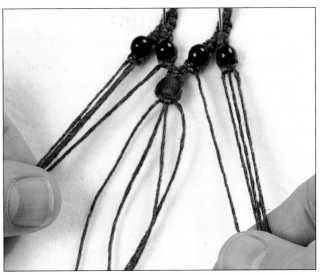

CREATING THE LOOP AND CLOSURE

1 Use a T-pin to anchor the group of threads with the slip-loop knot to the knotting board. Pick up one strand to use as the knotting strand. Hold the two remaining strands taut with the other hand. Tie 10 RDHHs with the single strand. Remove the T-pin from the board and pull out the slip-loop knot. Shape the knotted section into an arc, creating a group of six cords underneath. Use two outside strands to tie three SQKTs around the remaining four threads. This creates the loop for the necklace. Divide the six threads into three groups with two strands in each. Make a 9-inch (22.9 cm) three-ply braid with the strands. Finish the braid with three square knots. Set this unit aside.

Pick up the three strands with the single bead. Anchor the bead and strands to the knotting board with a single T-pin. Bring the strands together under the bead. Use two outer strands to tie three SQKTs around four knot-bearing strands. This creates the closure for the necklace. Divide the six threads into three groups with two strands in each. Make a 9-inch (22.9 cm) three-ply braid with the strands. Finish the braid with three SQKTS. Set this unit aside.

JOINING THE LOOP AND CLOSURE

2 Place the completed loop and closure about ½ inch (1.3 cm) apart on the knotting board. Anchor each with a T-pin. Divide the strands into four groups made up of three strands. Tie two SQKTs in each group. Thread a ³⁄₁₆-inch black bead on the knot-bearing strand of each group. Secure each bead in place with a SQKT.

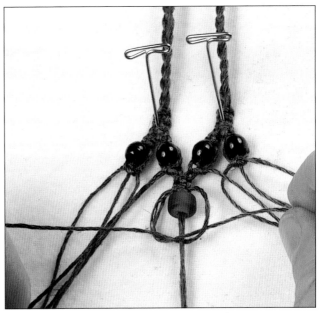

3 Divide the strands into three groups made up of four strands. Tie two SQKTs in each group. Thread one ¼-inch (6 mm) frosted-glass bead on the knot bearing strand of each group. Secure each bead in place with one SQKT below the bead. Make the two outside strands inactive on the right and left side. Regroup the remaining eight strands into two groups

of four. Tie one SQKT in each group. Make four outside strands on the left and right inactive, and tie one SQKT in the four remaining strands.

Tie two rows of DHHs diagonally below the square knots. Hold the outside strand on the left diagonally across five strands. Tie a row of DHHs using the five strands. Pick up the outside strand on the left and tie a second row of DHHs across four cords. Repeat this knotting sequence with the right-hand cords.

CREATING THE CENTRAL PENDANT

4 Begin working with the four strands in the center. Tie one SQKT. Thread a black glass pony bead onto the two knot-bearing strands. Secure the bead in place with one SQKT. Thread a frosted-glass bead on the two knot-bearing strands. Secure the bead with one SQKT. Thread a black glass pony bead on the knot-bearing strands and secure it in place with one SQKT.

Pick up two strands to the left of the unit you just tied. Tie 15 RDHH. Pick up the next two strands and tie 18 RDHH. Repeat this sequence with the four strands on the right.

Divide the strands used to tie the SQKT unit into two groups. Pick up the outermost strand in the left-hand group. Anchor the thread with a T-pin. Hold the strand diagonally over the threads in both RDHH units on the left. Tie a second row below the first using the

second strand from the center unit. Repeat this sequence on the right-hand side.

Locate and pick up the four strands in the center. Tie three SQKTs (see photo).

Two rows of DHHs are now tied to mirror the DHH rows described above. This creates a diamond-like outline around the SQKTs. Divide the strands in the SQKT unit into two groups, and tie double rows of DHHs.

5 Finish the necklace with three beaded units. Locate the four center strands. Tie one SQKT, and thread a frosted plum bead on the knot-bearing strands. Secure the bead with one SQKT. Thread a black pony bead onto the knot-bearing strands. Slide it into place and secure with one SQKT. Add one more black pony bead and secure with a SQKT. Tie an OK, pulling it up against the SQKT (see photo).

Work with four strands on the left. Tie one SQKT, thread a black pony bead and secure it in place with a SQKT. Add a second black pony bead and secure in place with a SQKT. Finish this unit with one OK. Trim the thread ends as desired. Repeat with the right-hand group.

Op! Eyeglass Case

If you tend to stuff your reading glasses in a satchel or throw them on the car seat, this case is just the ticket. Stylishly knotted in soft black and white cotton threads, this eyeglass case is—dare we say it?—a fine piece of knotted op(tical) art.

YOU WILL NEED

3 x 12-inch (7.6 x 30.5 cm) piece of heavy corrugated cardboard*

28 yards (25.6 m) of white, 4-ply, worsted weight 100% cotton yarn

28 yards (25.6 m) of black, 4-ply, worsted weight 100% cotton yarn

Decorative button, approximately ⅞ inch (2.2 cm) in diameter

Ruler or measuring tape

Scissors

Knotting board

T-pins

2 short lengths of any color yarn, each about 6 inches (15.2 cm) long

Tapestry or yarn needle

*Measure and cut this out of a corrugated box that you're planning to recycle.

DIMENSIONS OF FINISHED PIECE:
3 ⅝ x 7 inches (9.2 x 17.8 cm)

KNOTS AND WORKING METHOD
Lark's head knot (LHK), square knot (SQKT), slip-loop knot (SLK), reverse double half hitch (RDHH), overhand knot (OK)

Knotting in the round

Preparing the Materials

Measure and cut one 18-inch (45.7 cm) length of white yarn for a mounting cord. Measure and cut two pieces of black yarn 24 inches (70 cm) long for the closure. Set them aside.

Measure and cut 18 strands of white cotton yarn, each 54 inches (1.4 m) long. Measure and cut 18 strands of black cotton yarn, each 54 inches (1.4 m) long.

Center one 18-inch (45.7 cm) length of white cotton yarn across the short width of the cardboard strip. Bring the ends around the strip and back to the front. Tie the two ends together with a single SQKT. Position the tied cord approximately 3 inches (7.6 cm) from the top of the strip. This is your anchor cord. Pin the cardboard form to your knotting board with T-pins.

2 Pick up four white threads. Tie a SQKT. Tie a SQKT in the next group of threads. As you continue to knot the row around the form, you will need to remove the pins, turn the form over, and pin it again. Continue around the form.

1 Fold one 54-inch (1.4 m) length of white cotton yarn in half. Mount the yarn on the holding strand using a LHK. Mount a second length of white yarn in the same way. Mount two lengths of black cotton yarn on the holding strand with LHKs. Continue mounting yarn in pairs: two white and two black. You will mount cords over the SQKT you tied in the anchor cord. Remove the pins to turn the cardboard. You should mount 18 units on each side. Clip the loose ends of the anchor cord as needed.

3 After you have completed the first row, you will need to regroup threads. Pick up two white and two black threads. Tie one SQKT. Continue around the form, regrouping and tying SQKTs. Tie eight rows of alternating, single SQKTs.

Row 9 will be knotted with two SQKTs in each group of four threads. Row 10 is tied with single SQKTs. Repeat rows 9 and 10 two times.

The remainder of the case will be knotted in alternating rows of single SQKT. Tie 28 rows of alternating SQKTs.

FINISHING THE CASE

4 Identify the four strands at each side of the case (two white and two black). Tie a short length of red yarn around each of the four strands of yarn. Bend the cardboard a bit, slide the case off the form, and turn it inside out. Slip the case back onto the form. Slide the case down until the last row of knotting is even with the edge of the form. Comb the threads with your fingers, letting them fall to the side of the pouch where they originate. Make sure that the cords you marked with the red yarn thread are on the side edges of the form. The bottom of the pouch will be tied off using square knots without a knot-bearing cord. The marked side strands will be tied last. Pick up a pair of threads from each side of the form next to one of the marked pairs. Tie one SQKT (see photo). Pull it securely against the cardboard edge. Pick up the next pair of threads and tie a SQKT. Continue across, picking up matching pairs in order until all are tied. Remove the red yarn and tie each pair in a SQKT. Trim the thread ends to ¼ inch (6mm) with scissors.

5 Turn the case inside out. This is best done by pushing against the bottom with your thumbs while you begin to pull down the sides. Be sure you push out the bottom corners with your fingers, before the case is fully turned.

CREATING THE CLOSURE

6 Use a 6-inch (15.2 cm) length of black yarn to attach a button on the front of the case. Thread the yarn through the holes or shank of the button. Pull the ends even and center the button on the thread. Tie a SQKT. Locate the center knot on one side of the case. Thread one end of the yarn in the tapestry needle.

Bring the end through the case to one side of the center knot (see photo on page 49). Unthread the needle and repeat with the other yarn end. Tie one SQKT with the thread ends on the inside of the case. Finish with a tightly made OK. Trim the yarn ends.

7 Pick up two 24-inch (70 cm) black yarn strands. Secure both strands together at their midpoint with a SLK. Pin the knot to the knotting board. Tie 20 RDHH.

9 Thread two of the strands in the needle. Identify the center knot in row 3 on the back of the case. Pull the strands to the inside of the case on one side of the knot. Repeat with the other two strands. Tie one SQKT with the four strands. Finish with one OK in each pair.

8 Remove the slip loop knot. Bring the four strands together creating a loop. Pin the loop to the knotting board. Tie eight SQKT.

Key Ring Pouch

Slip everything into this pouch and travel light. Keys on the ring, cash, and one or two important plastic cards stashed inside are all you'll need.

**DIMENSIONS OF
FINISHED PIECE**
2 ½ x 3 ½ inches (6.4 x 8.9 cm)

YOU WILL NEED

2 x 7-inch (5 x 17.8 cm) piece of
heavy corrugated cardboard*

Metal O-ring, approximately ½ inch
(1.3 cm) in diameter

Metal split-ring

82 feet (24.9 m) of oatmeal-colored,
cotton quick crochet thread

82 feet (24.9 m) of blue, cotton
quick crochet thread

Ruler or measuring tape

Scissors

Knotting board

T-pins

Tapestry needle

*Measure and cut out a piece of a
corrugated box that you're planning
to recycle.

KNOTS AND WORKING METHOD
Lark's head knot (LHK), square knot
(SQKT), double half hitch (DHH)

Knotting in the round

Preparing the materials

Measure and cut three pieces of oatmeal thread, each 3 feet (91 cm) long. Measure and cut 18 pieces of oatmeal thread, each 4 feet (1.2 m) long. Measure and cut 18 pieces of blue thread, each 4 feet (1.2 m) long.

Anchor the O-ring to the knotting board with a T-pin. Fold each 3-foot length of oatmeal thread in half. Mount each thread on the ring using LHKs. You will have six knotting strands. Tie four SQKTs around four knot-bearing threads.

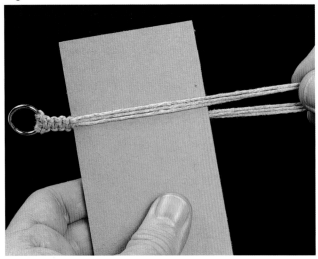

1 Remove the O-ring from the knotting board. Slip the cardboard strip between the oatmeal threads, as shown in the photo. Make sure you have three threads on each side. The cardboard strip becomes a form to separate the sides of the pouch as you knot. Wrap the thread ends back around to the SQKTs. These threads are your anchor strand.

2 Hold the cardboard form between your knees with the O-ring toward your body. Pick up single strands from each side and use them as knotting strands. Tie four SQKTs around all the strands including the first sinnet of SQKTs that you tied.

3 Thread the tapestry needle with one knotting thread end. Push the needle back under the SQKTs and pull the thread through. Repeat with the other thread. Trim the excess thread ends.

4 Lay the form down on your knotting board with the O-ring on the left. Pick up one of the long blue threads. Fold it in half at midpoint. Mount the folded thread onto the anchor strand with a LHK. Mount a second blue thread in the same way. Mount two oatmeal threads with LHKs. Continue mounting all of the long threads in alternating pairs of color around the

cardboard form. When all threads have been mounted, check your pattern. Do you have alternating pairs of color? If you don't, fix the pattern now! Move any misplaced colors as needed.

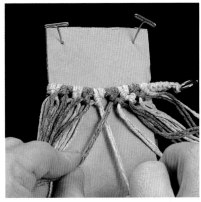

6 The O-ring is now on the right. Regroup the strands to begin the second row. Work toward the left, with the strand on the right held over the left. Use one pair of blue and one pair of oatmeal strands to tie one DHH. Work around the cardboard form.

You will tie 24 rows in all, regrouping as each row is completed, and working back toward where you started each time.

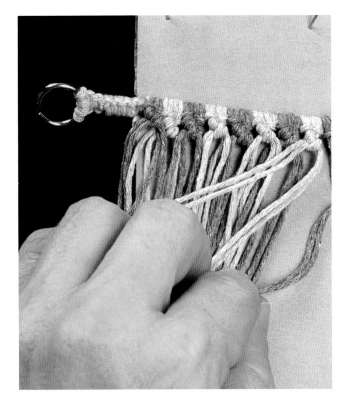

FINISHING THE POUCH

7 Tie a short length of a contrasting thread color around the double strands at each bottom corner of the cardboard form (see photo). Bend the cardboard a bit, and slide the pouch off the form. Turn the pouch inside out. Slip the pouch back onto the form. Slide the pouch down until the last row of knotting is even with the edge of the form.

Comb the threads with your fingers, letting them fall to the side of the pouch where they originated. Make sure that the cords you marked with contrasting thread are at the corners again. The bottom of the pouch will be finished with SQKTs tied without knot-bearing cords. The marked side strands will be the last to be tied.

5 You'll work with two pairs of thread at a time to create this design. It looks complicated, but it isn't. If you pay attention to the pattern's color changes, any mistake you make will jump out at you and can be easily fixed. Start with the ring on the left and work to the right. Hold the first double blue strand across the adjacent double blue strand. Tie a DHH with the right strand around the left. Pick up the next double oatmeal strand, hold it across the next oatmeal strands and tie one DHH with the right strand around the left. Continue knotting around the form until you arrive back at the O-ring. All pairs of strands will have been knotted.

Pick up a pair of threads from each side of the form starting at a marked double strand. Tie one SQKT. Pull it securely against the cardboard edge. Pick up the next pair of threads and tie a SQKT. Continue across, picking up matching pairs until all are tied. Remove the contrasting threads and tie each pair in a SQKT. Trim the thread ends with scissors. Turn the pouch inside out. Poke the corners out with your fingertips.

Slip the split-key ring onto the O-ring.

Sands of Time Watchband

Timeless…that's how to describe the style of this finely knotted watchband. For him or for her!

YOU WILL NEED

Watchband buckle

40 feet (12.2 m) of waxed nylon thread

Ruler or tape measure

Scissors

Knotting board

T-pins

Clear-drying white craft glue

**DIMENSIONS
OF FINISHED PIECE**

9 inches (22.9 cm) in length

KNOTS AND WORKING METHOD

Square knot (SQKT), reverse double half hitch (RDHH),
lark's head knot (LHK), double half hitch (DHH)

Working from one end

Preparing the Materials

Measure and cut four strands, each 8 feet (2.4 m) long. Measure and cut two strands, each 2 feet (61 cm) long. Set the shorter strands to the side.

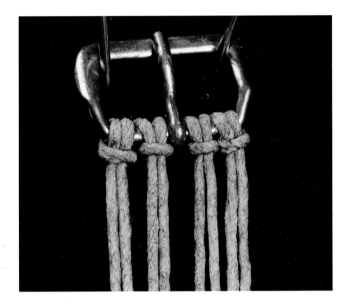

1 Find the midpoint of one long strand. Fold it in half and mount it on the buckle bar with a LHK. Mount the remaining long strands in the same way. Make sure you have two sets on either side of the tongue. Secure the buckle to the knotting board with t-pins.

Divide the strands in two groups. Tie one SQKT in each group. Make two strands inactive on each side. Tie a SQKT in the center group of four. Repeat this alternating SQKT pattern six times. You will have knotted 14 rows in all.

2 Pick up an outside strand from the left side. Tie two diagonal rows of DHH below the square knots. Repeat this step on the opposite side.

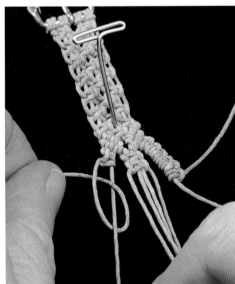

Pick up the four strands in the center and tie two SQKTs. Use the two outer strands on the right to tie six RDHHs. Tie six RDHHs on the left side (see photo).

Working with the fourth strand from the left side, hold it diagonally downward to the left across three strands and tie DHHs. Repeat, again using the fourth strand from the left. Repeat this pattern of DHHs on the right side.

3 Pick up the four strands in the middle, and tie one SQKT. Regroup all of the strands into two groups of four. Tie one SQKT in each group. Repeat the two rows of SQKTs twice.

Think of the strands (counting from the left) as numbers one through eight. Allow strands 1 and 2 to be inactive. Combine strands 3 and 4 with strands 5 and 6, tie one SQKT. Allow strands 1, 2, 3, and 4 to be inactive. Combine strands 5 and 6 with strands 7 and 8, and tie one SQKT. Repeat this sequence in reverse order to the left, then back to the right.

Using the four middle strands tie one SQKT. Regroup eight strands into two groups of four; tie one SQKT in each group. Repeat this sequence twice. Tie one SQKT using the four center strands.

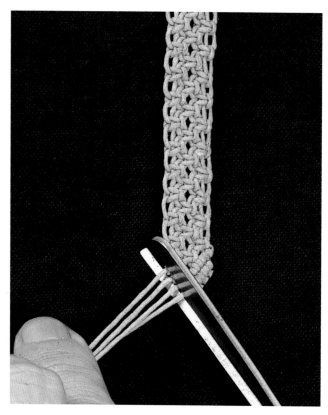

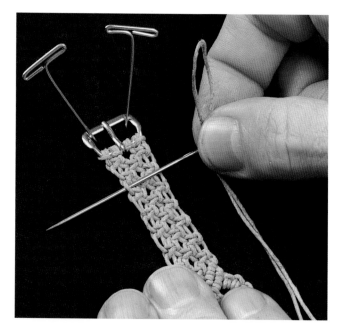

4 Repeat the design pattern in step 2. You will end with two rows of DHHs.

Pick up the four center threads. Tie a SQKT. Then tie 26 rows of alternating SQKTs. You will have 27 rows of SQKTs in all.

Pick up the outside strand on either side. Tie a diagonal row of DHH using three strands. Tie a second row in the same direction. Repeat on the opposite side, bringing the band to a point.

Connect the two sides of the watchband point. Hold the last knot bearing cord over the fourth strand in the opposite group. Tie a DHH using this strand. Trim the thread ends close to the knotting. Spread a small amount of clear drying white craft glue on the ends. Allow the glue to dry.

ADDING THE LOOPS TO THE WATCHBAND

5 Pick up a 2-foot (61 cm) strand. Fold it in half at the midpoint. Thread the loop into a tapestry needle. Count four rows down from the bottom of the buckle. You should end on a single SQKT. Bring the threaded needle under the left-hand outside strand, and pull the loop through.

6 Use a LHK to anchor the long strand to the inactive strand to the left of the SQKT.

Anchor the second strand to the band two rows down from the first.

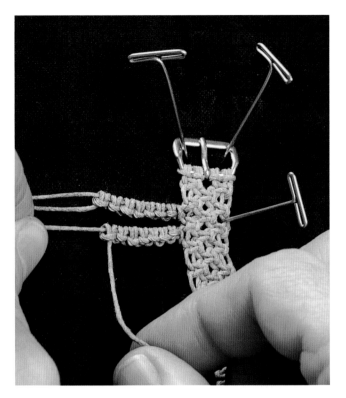

7 Tie seven RDHHs in each pair of strands.

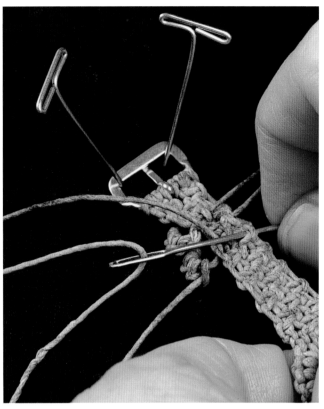

9 Turn the watchband over. Work with one unit at a time. Thread the one free strand in the needle. Pull the strand under the back loop of one of the SQKTs. Repeat with each strand. Clip the strands closely. Cover the clipped ends with clear-drying white craft glue. Allow the glue to dry before you proudly slip your watch onto your wrist!

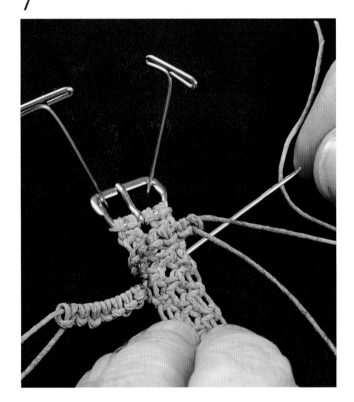

8 Work with one unit at a time. Bring the knot-bearing strand of each unit to the side opposite where you anchored the strands. Thread the strand between the two inactive strands and pull it to the back of the band. Repeat with the second unit.

Over-the-Shoulder Water Bottle Tote

Life is a juggling act and you've only got two hands. Why should toting life's necessities—cell phone, briefcase, gym bag, and perhaps a toddler as well—be complicated with one more thing? When you knot this tote you'll give yourself an extra hand, and quick access to a much needed swig of water!

DIMENSIONS
OF FINISHED PIECE
22 inches (55.9 cm) in length

YOU WILL NEED

180 feet (54.9 m) of cotton cable cord

2 metal O-rings, each approximately 1 inch (2.54 cm) in diameter

Scissors

Ruler or measuring tape

T-pins

Rubber bands

Masking tape

Knotting board

Water bottle*

*You start the knotting for this project on the knotting board, and then move to knotting directly around your water bottle. Make sure your bottle is filled with water to provide a sturdy surface to work on.

KNOTS AND WORKING METHOD
Lark's head knot (LHK), square knot (SQKT), half hitch (HH), double half hitch (DHH), overhand knot (OK)

Knotting in the round and from one end

Preparing the Materials

Measure and cut 18 pieces of cotton cable cord, each 10 feet (3.1 m) long. Locate the midpoint of one strand, fold it in half, and mount it onto one of the O-rings with a LHK. Mount all 18 strands with LHKs. Anchor the O-ring to the knotting board with a few T-pins.

1 Fan out the cords on the knotting board. Separate the cords into groups of four. Tie a sinnet of eight SQKTs in each group. Remove the T-pins.

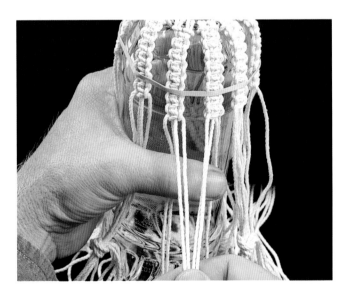

2 Turn your filled water bottle upside-down. Center the O-ring on the bottom of the bottle. Secure the knotted sinnets to the bottle with a rubber band. Once the rubber band is in place, space the sinnets evenly around the bottle.

Divide the four cords in one sinnet into groups of two. Tie two AHHs in each set of two. Repeat with each group of cords around the bottle.

3 Regroup the cords into groups of four, using two cords from adjacent sinnets of AHHs. Tie two SQKTs. Tie the first half of a SQKT, but do not pull it tight. Leave approximately a ¾-inch (1.9 cm) space. Use a T-pin to hold the space open.

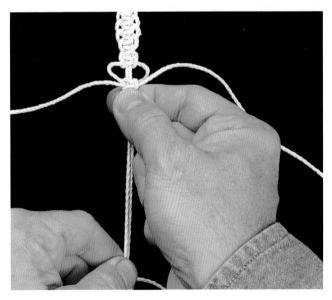

4 Complete the second half of the SQKT. Remove the T-pin and slide the knot-bearing cords up against the first half of the SQKT. This creates decorative loops. Finish the sinnet with a SQKT pulled tight against the previous SQKTs. Repeat this knotting sequence around the bottle.

Divide each group of four cords into two groups and tie two AHHs in each set.

Regroup two cords from adjacent units into groups of four, and tie a sinnet of five SQKTS. Repeat this sequence around the bottle.

Regroup the cords into groups of two, and tie two AHH in each group around the bottle.

5 Regroup the cords into groups of four. Tie two SQKTs, tie a SQKT with a decorative loop, and finish the sinnet with a SQKT. Repeat this sequence around the bottle.

Regroup the four-strand units into two groups of two, and tie two AHHs with each group.

Regroup the cords a final time into groups of four. Tie three SKQTs in each group around the bottle. This is the last part of the design that will be worked around the bottle.

6 Group three SQKT sinnets together. This will create a group with 12 strands. Regroup the 12 cords: eight cords in the center, two inactive on each side. Divide the eight cords into two groups of four. Tie one SQKT in each group. Regroup again, two inactive on each side. Tie one SKQT with the four cords in the center.

Now, divide the 12 cords into two groups of six. Beginning on the left or right, anchor the outside strand, and hold it across five cords. Tie DHHs with the five cords. Tie a second row below the first. Repeat the two rows of DHHs on the opposite side.

Tie a row of GDHH on the left and right sides (see photo). Review GDHH on page 17 if needed. Start on either side. Anchor the outside strand, hold it across the remaining cords in the group, and tie a DHH with the second strand. Continue until all six cords are used on this side.

Repeat this step around the bottle with the remaining SQKT sinnets.

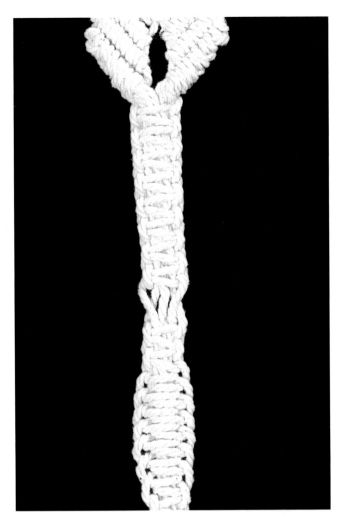

7 Identify the last cord used on the left and right in the final row of GDHHs. Use these two strands as knotting cords, and tie two SQKTs around 10 cords.

Comb the strands below the SQKTs with your fingers. Select any two of the shorter strands, and trim them just below the SQKT. Tie two more SQKTs, and cut out two more cords. Tie two more SKQTs and cut two more cords. You will have removed six cords in all.

Select two long cords from the center and move them to each side. They will be your knotting strands. Tie two SQKTs.

Tie 14 AHHs using two outside strands around four knot-bearing strands. Move the knotting strands to the center, and select two long cords from the center and move them to each side. Tie two SQKT.

Select and cut the two shortest knot-bearing strands right below the last SQKT. Tie one SQKT.

Tie 12 AHH using single knotting strands around two knot-bearing strands. Finish with two SQKT.

8 Start a SQKT. Create a decorative loop as you did in step 3. Tie one SQKT.

Exchange the inner and outer cords. Tie three SQKT.

Attach this unit to an O-ring. Place the two knotting strands under the ring and the two knot-bearing strands over the ring. Tie two SQKTs. Use all four strands to tie an OK. Trim the cord ends.

Repeat step 7 and step 8 around the bottle.

To Market, To Market Bag

When the clerk asks you: "Paper or plastic?" respond with a simple, "Neither, thank you. I have my own!" Make your last minute shopping stops with this stylishly knotted bag to eliminate (or at least lessen) your collection of plastic shopping bags.

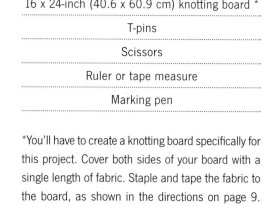

DIMENSIONS OF FINISHED PIECE

14 x 30 inches (35.6 x 76.2 cm)

YOU WILL NEED

192 yards (175.6 m) natural hemp cord

2 bamboo handbag rings, approximately 5 inches (12.7 cm) in diameter

16 x 24-inch (40.6 x 60.9 cm) knotting board *

T-pins

Scissors

Ruler or tape measure

Marking pen

*You'll have to create a knotting board specifically for this project. Cover both sides of your board with a single length of fabric. Staple and tape the fabric to the board, as shown in the directions on page 9.

KNOTS AND WORKING METHOD

Lark's head knot (LHK) , square knot (SQKT), double half hitch (DHH), overhand knot (OK), coil knot (CK)

Knotting from one end and in the round

Preparing the Materials

Measure and cut 6-yard (5.5 m) lengths of hemp. You will need 32 lengths in all. Find the midpoint of each strand and fold it in half. Use LHKs to mount 16 strands on each bamboo ring.

Use T-pins to secure one bamboo ring to each side of the knotting board. The top of each ring should be pinned approximately 1 inch (2.5 cm) from the top edge of the board. Comb and separate the cords with your fingers to place them in order.

1 You may start on either side of the board. Pick up two outer strands on the right. Tie 20 AHHs and place the unit aside. Pick up the adjacent unit of four strands. Tie three SQKTs (see photo).

Exchange the knotting strands with the knot bearing strands. Exchanging strands will create an open space. With the strands in a new position, tie three SQKTs. Exchange the strands again, and tie three SQKTs. Place this unit aside.

2 Pick up the next unit of four strands; tie three SQKTs. Exchange the knotting strands with the knot bearing strands. Tie three SQKTs, and place this unit aside. Pick up the next unit of four strands. Tie

three SQKT, and place this unit aside. Pick up the next unit of four strands and tie two SQKTs. This becomes your center unit. Place this unit aside.

The cords remaining are knotted in reverse order from the center unit of two SQKTs. (You will have one unit of three SQKTs; a unit of SQKT with one strand exchange; and a unit with two strand exchanges.) The last two strands will be tied with 20 AHHs.

Turn the knotting board over and knot the other side following steps 1 and 2.

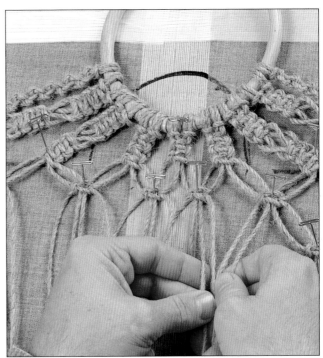

3 Use a marking pen to mark at the bottom of the center unit of two SQKTs. Measure from the mark to the top of the board. Use this measurement to mark two points on each side of the board. Draw a parallel line across the board using a ruler to make a straight line. Spread the strands evenly across the width of the board. Anchor the end of the knotted portion of the strands with T-pins close to the marked line (see photo).

The body of the shopping bag is created with a simple pattern of alternating SQKTs. Knots will be spaced approximately 1 inch (2.54 cm) apart. Begin knotting on either side of the board. Regroup the strands across and tie a single SQKT in each group. Secure each knot with a T-pin to maintain spacing. Turn the board over, and knot the opposite side in the same way. Regroup the strands again. This time the two outer strands on each side of the board will be grouped with two strands from the other side. Tie one SQKT in each side group. Secure the SQKT to the edge of the board with a T-pin. Now, tie one SQKT in each group of four strands across the board. Repeat on the opposite side. As you work down the board, move your T-pins from one knot to the next. Otherwise, you'll need a lot of T-pins

Knot 18 rows of alternating SQKTs on each side. Your last row should occur near the bottom of the board.

CLOSING THE BAG

4 Locate the SQKT pinned to the side of the board in the last row. Divide the four strands into two groups of two. Tie six AHHs in each group of two. Start from the left and hold the first strand from the AHH across the four strands of the adjacent SQKT. Tie DHHs using all four strands.

5 Hold the second strand from the AHH unit across the four strands just used and tie a second row of DHHs.

Repeat steps 4 and 5 with the cords on the right side. Then, turn the board over and repeat on the left and right as just described.

6 The remainder of the bag bottom will be tied off with combination of SQKTs and OKs. Work from either the left or the right. Pick up two corresponding strands from each side of the bag. Tie one SQKT without a knot-bearing strand. Continue tying SQKTs across the bottom of the bag until all strands have been used and the bottom is joined.

7 Tie one OK using the four strands that you used to tie a SQKT. Pull the knot up snugly against the SQKT.

8 Tie a CK about 2 inches (5 cm) below the OK in each strand. Use scissors to trim the strands as desired.

Seafarer's Sampler

Ahoy, matey! Macrame projects don't always have to be functional. Inspired by the knot samplers tied by nineteenth century seafarers, which are eagerly collected as folk art today, this project will show off your knotting prowess.

DIMENSIONS OF FINISHED PIECE

5 x 6 inches (12.7 x 15.2 cm

YOU WILL NEED

90 feet (27.4 m) of medium cotton cable cord

Ruler or measuring tape

Scissors

Knotting board

T-pins

Paper clamps

Clear-drying white craft glue

KNOTS AND WORKING METHOD

Slip-loop knot (SLK), lark's head knot (LHK), square knot (SQKT), half knot (HK), reverse double half hitch (RDHH), double half hitch (DHH), overhand knot (OK)

Knotting from one end

Preparing the Materials

Measure and cut two cords each 8 feet (2.4 m) long. Measure and cut 16 pieces of cord each 5 feet (1.5 m) long.

1 Grasp the two 8-foot (2.4 m) pieces at the midpoint. Tie a SLK about 4 inches (10.2 cm) from each side of the midpoint. This becomes your anchor strand. Place T-pins through each SLK to hold the anchor strand to the knotting board. Double each 5-foot (1.5 m) cord at the midpoint. Mount each cord with a LHK to the holding strand. Wind the cord ends of the anchor strand and secure them with paper clamps.

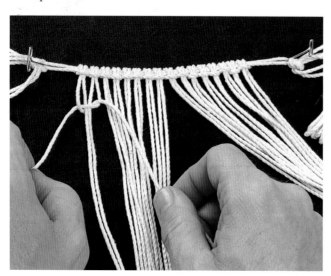

2 Divide the cords into two groups of 16 cords. Divide the left group into four groups of four cords. Tie one SQKT with each group. Regroup with two inactive cords on the left and right. Tie one SQKT in each group of four. Knot five rows of alternating SQKTs in all.

Divide the 16 strands on the right into groups of four. Tie a sinnet of five SQKTs with the four strands on the right and the left side of this half. Tie HKs in each of the two middle groups of four.

3 Remove the T-pin on the left side of the anchor cord. Pin the upper left SQKT. Remove the paper clamp and the slip loop knot in the anchor strand. Use the left strand as the knotting strand; the right one as the knot-bearing strand. Tie five RDHH. Place a T-pin in the fifth RDHH.

4 Lay the outside strand (below the RDHH) across 17 strands as a knot-bearing cord. Tie DHHs with the 17 strands. Place a T-pin in the last DHH and turn the knot-bearing cord back to the left. Tie a second row of DHHs using all 17 strands around the knot bearing cord. You will have two strands hanging on the

left side. Re-bundle those cords with the paper clamp.

Repeat step 3 and step 4 (up to this point) with the right half of the sampler.

Now, divide the 32 strands into groups as follows: a group of four, three groups of eight cords and a group of four (4,8,8,8,4). Tie a sinnet of five SQKT with each group of four on the left and right sides.

Locate the center group of eight strands. Use a T-pin to anchor both of the two center strands in the group. Hold the pinned strand on the left diagonally to the left. Tie a row of DHH with the remaining three strands in that half of the group. Repeat this with the right strand.

Anchor the knot-bearing cords you just used (now located on the outside of this group of eight). Working with one strand at a time, hold each at a diagonal. Tie a row of DHHs with each strand creating a diamond motif. Tie one SQKT using the four strands below the diamond you just created.

Repeat the diamond motif using the remaining groups of eight on the left and right. Tie one SQKT under each diamond.

Remove the paper clamp from the inactive cords on each side. Tie five RDHHs on each side of the sampler as you did in step 3. Place a T-pin in the fifth RDHH on each side.

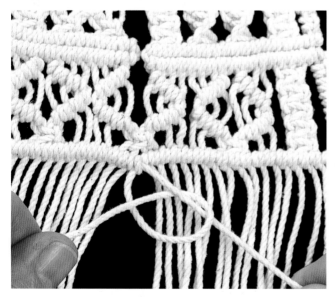

5 Holding the outside single strand across to the middle, tie 17 DHHs. Repeat on the opposite side of where you began. Pick up the knot-bearing cord coming from the left and continue across to the right

side with 17 DHH. Repeat this with the knot-bearing cord coming from the right side, knotting 17 DHH to the left. The two sides are now connected. Clamp the two holding cords on each side and make them inactive.

6 Separate the strands into two groups of 16 each. Work first with the 16 strands on the right. Pick up the center four strands and tie one SQKT, pulling it up against the row of DHHs. Regroup the strands, picking up two on the right and left, and combine with two each from the SQKT. Tie one SQKT in each group. Regroup again, moving to the right and left; tie one SQKT in each. Regroup one final time, and tie one SQKT in each group of four. You have created an inverted V-shape made up of seven SQKT.

Knot with the 16 strands on the left side. Tie one SQKT in each of the outer groups of four. Pull in place against DHH rows. Regroup, picking up the new two cords beside each square knot; tie one SQKT in each new group. (The square knot will go no higher than the previous knot.) Regroup and tie one SQKT on the right and left. Regroup and tie one SQKT with the middle four. You have an inverted image of the right hand side.

Remove the clamp from the inactive bundles; working with the two strands, left and right, tie four RDHH in each set. Anchor the outside cords and create DHH rows as you did in step 3.

7 The bottom section is almost a repeat of the first section in step 2. Work with groups of 16 cords. Be sure you don't include the holding cords in these groups. In the right-hand group, tie seven rows of alternating SQKTs.

In the left-hand group, tie two SQKT sinnets on each side of the group. The sinnets are made with seven SQKTs. In the center, tie two spiraling HK sinnets with 14 HKs in each.

8 Tie eight RDHH with each pair of holding cords. Anchor the outside strands of each set of holding cords. One at a time, bring each cord across 16 strands. Tie a row of 16 DHHs. On each side, anchor the second holding cord, and tie a second row of 16 DHHs.

Gather the four holding cords in the center and tie an OK. Pull it snugly. Trim the cords below the OK with scissors as desired. Trim the remaining cord ends just below the DHHs. Dab a bit of white craft glue on the trimmed ends to reduce raveling.

Use tiny tacks, stitching, or glue to mount the finished sampler in a deep shadow-box frame.

Wired-Up Bracelet

Forget traditional knotting materials! This bracelet lets you explore new knotting dimensions using colored wires. Yes, wires. It's a little tricky, but the result is well worth the effort. When you've practiced with craft wires, move on to fine gauge sterling silver or gold wires.

DIMENSIONS OF FINISHED PIECE

9 inches (22.9 cm) in length

YOU WILL NEED

8 feet (2.4 m) of 22-gauge colored craft wire in the color of your choice*

10 feet (3 m) of 24-gauge gold-colored craft wire

2 large pony beads

16 small pony beads

2 round focus beads, about $\frac{3}{8}$ inch (9.5 mm) in diameter

4 round opaque beads, $\frac{3}{16}$ inch (5 mm) in diameter

8 gold-plated E beads

Ruler or tape measure

Wire cutters or scissors

Knotting board

T-pins

Jewelry pliers (flat or round-nose)

*Craft stores now stock a wide selection of colored craft wire. This bracelet is knotted with a powder blue wire; the beads were chosen to complement it. Let yourself be seduced (but not overwhelmed) by the variety of colors you'll find. Choose two fabulous focus beads for the central portion of the design before you select the rest of the beads for the bracelet.

KNOTS AND WORKING METHOD
Square knot (SQKT), half hitch (HH), alternating half hitch (AHH)

Knotting from one end

Preparing the Materials

Measure and cut two pieces of colored wire, each 4 feet (1.2 m) long. Measure and cut two pieces of gold-colored wire, each 5 feet (1.5 m) long.

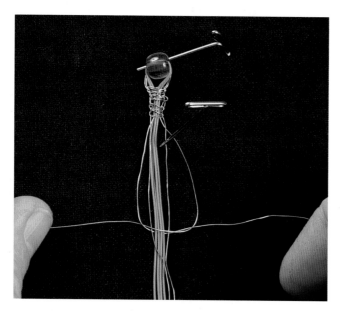

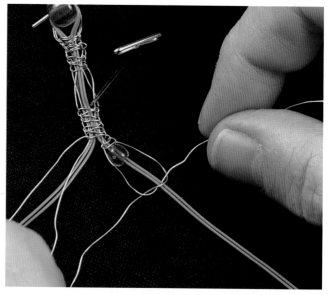

1 Thread one large pony bead onto all four wire strands. Slide the bead to the midpoint of the strands. Bend the wires down around the bead. Use a T-pin to secure the bead and wires to the knotting board. Use two gold-colored wires to tie four SQKTs around the remaining wires. Pick up the gold wires used as knot-bearing wires. Move them to the outside. Place the knotting wires (just used) parallel to the colored wires.

Place a T-pin about ¼ inch (6 mm) below the first group of SQKTs. Tie four SQKTs. Bring the first knot up to the T-pin. This will form a space between the groups of knots.

2 Divide the wires into two groups with two colored and two gold wires in each group. Tie one SQKT with the gold wires in each group. Thread one small pony bead onto both colored wires of each group. Tie one SQKT below the bead with the gold strands. Add two more beads to each group, securing each bead with a SQKT. You will have added six small pony beads in all.

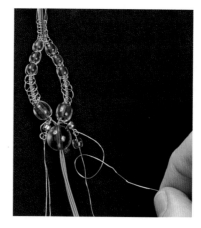

3 Knot one group with eight AHHs using the gold wires around the colored wire. Knot the opposite group. Tie one SQKT below the series of AHH. Thread a ³⁄₁₆-inch (5 mm) bead onto the colored wires of each unit. Secure each bead with one SQKT. Thread all four colored wires through a ³⁄₈-inch (9.5 mm) focus bead.

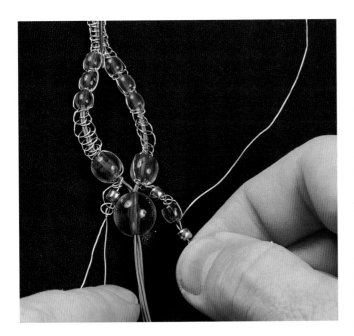

Bring the two knotted units in step 2 together. Tie three SQKT using two gold wires as knotting wires, six wires remaining. Exchange the gold knotting strands with the gold knot bearing wires.

4 Now, work with two gold strands on either side. Tie two HH using one gold wire as the knotting wire, the other as knot-bearing. Thread one gold E bead onto the knot-bearing wire. Tie two more HH and thread a small pony bead on the knot-bearing wire. Thread one gold E bead onto the knot-bearing wire. Tie two more HH. Repeat this on the opposite side.

6 Divide the wires into two groups. Make sure you have two gold and two colored wires in each group. Tie seven SQKT with the gold wires in each group. Use your fingers to form each group into a half circle.

Bring the ends of the wires together. Tie three SQKTs, using gold wire as knotting strands. Thread a large pony bead on all eight wires. Push the bead snugly up against the knots. Use the jewelry pliers to twist the strands together. Trim the ends of the wires to about ¼ inch (6 mm). A dab of white craft glue on the wire ends will protect you from the sharp edges. Shape the finished bracelet on your wrist.

Slip the bead into the loop to fasten the bracelet.

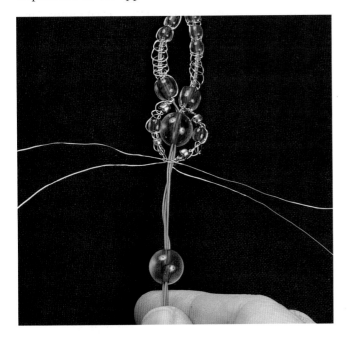

5 Tie one SQKT with the single knot-bearing gold wires (on the left and right) around the blue wires below the focus bead.

Create a mirror image of the design from where the wires split into two units of four strands each. First, repeat step 4; then, repeat steps 3 and 2.

Baroque Brooch

Elaborate brooches and the art of macrame were both passions of the Victorians in the nineteenth century. Crafting mourning jewelry of knotted hairwork combined the two passions and was extremely popular. This stunning project is a more colorful (and far easier to knot) homage to that peculiar craft.

DIMENSIONS OF THE FINISHED PIECE

1½ x 7 inches (3.8 x 17.8 cm) including the fringe

YOU WILL NEED

20 feet (6.1 m) of waxed linen thread

30 small round black beads, ⅛ inch (3 mm) in diameter

2 focus beads, ⅜ inch (9.5 mm) in diameter*

1 focus bead, ¾ inch (1.9 cm) in diameter*

Ruler or measuring tape

Scissors

Pin clasp

Paper clamps

Knotting board

T-pins

*These beads will be featured prominently in your brooch. Select them with that in mind. If you can't find three beads exactly alike, don't despair. Choose a focus bead and two smaller beads to complement it.

KNOTS AND WORKING METHOD

Overhand knot (OK), half hitch (HH), square knot (SQKT), reverse double half hitch (RDHH), coil knot (CK), double half hitch (DHH), gathering double half hitch (GDHH)

Knotting from one end

Preparing the Materials

Measure and cut four threads, each 30 inches (76.2 cm) long. Measure and cut four threads, each 24 inches (61 cm) long.

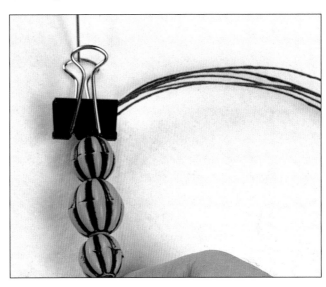

1 Thread four 30-inch (76.2 cm) threads through the three focus beads. Use a paper clamp to hold the threads together 12 inches (30.5 cm) from the end. Push the beads against the clamp and tie one OK. Remove the clamp, and tie one OK at the opposite end of the beads.

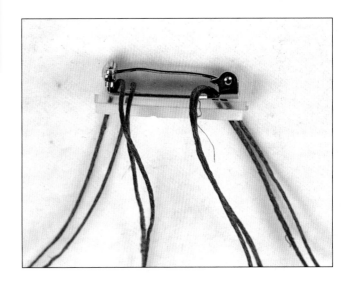

2 Thread two 24-inch (61 cm) threads at each end under the pin of the pin clasp. Turn the pin clasp face up.

doesn't matter which unit you start with. Combine it with the closest beaded strand tied with HHs. The strands with RDHHs will be knot-bearing and you will tie DHHs using the beaded HH strands. Now you have four strands to use for knotting.

Use three knot-bearing strands and one knotting strand. Tie eight RDHHs. Repeat this sequence on the opposite side.

3 Place the threaded focus beads on the clasp. Make sure that you have equal lengths of the 24-inch (61 cm) threads on either side of the clasp. Tie one SQKT with one set of the 24-inch (61 cm) threads between two beads, securing them to the clasp. Repeat with the remaining strands. These threads will be inactive for the present.

Divide the threads passing through the focus beads into sets of two. Tie one RDHH in each group. String one small black bead onto the knot-bearing strand of each set. Pull each bead into place against the RDHH. Then, tie six RDHH with each set of threads. These two sets will be inactive for a time.

Work with the four thread pairs that attached the focus beads to the pin clasp. Tie two HH in each pair. Thread a small round bead onto the two threads of each pair.

5 Now work with the remaining unknotted strands that hold the focus beads to the pin clasp. Thread a small bead onto one strand. Secure the bead with a DHH.

Pick up the RDHH strands from step 5. Combine them with the beaded DHH strands you just tied. The RDHH strands will be knot-bearing. Tie one DHH with the two strands as you did in step 5. You will have a group of six strands. Repeat this on the opposite side.

4 Now work with the threads in the focus bead unit. Pick up one of the units tied with RDHHs. It

6 Divide one group of six strands into a group of two and a group of four. Thread three small beads onto one strand in the group of two. Slip a bead up one strand and secure it snugly by tying a RDHH with the second strand. Secure the remaining two beads in the same way. Repeat this step with the other group of six strands. Both of these two-strand units will be inactive for a time.

7 Now work with one of the four-strand units. Tie six AHHs using double strands. Repeat with the opposite four-strand unit. These strands are now inactive for a time.

8 Work with the four unknotted strands at the base of the focus beads. Pick up one of the two center strands. Hold it across the adjacent outer strand to the left or right. Tie one DHH.

Bring this knot-bearing strand across the six-strand unit in step 7. Tie a row of DHHs using all six strands. The knot bearing strand will not hang down like the others so it will be easy to identify later (see photo).

Pick up the first strand hanging down from the row of DHHs. Hold it across five strands. Tie a row of DHH, but do not include the knotting strand you used previously. (That's why we said it would be easy to identify!)

Continue to work rows of DHHs picking up a strand, and holding it over the remaining strands. You will knot decreasing rows of DHHs. This process will create a triangular shape.

Create decreasing rows of DHH on the opposite side starting with the center strand.

All strands are going to be drawn down under the point of the triangle using GDHH. Work with one side of the design at a time.

Pick up the uppermost strand on one side of the triangle shape. Hold it down and across the strands. Tie one DHH. Combine the two strands; pick up the next free knotting strand and tie one DHH. Continue combining strands and tying DHHs in this manner until all the strands on one side of the design hang under the point in the center. Repeat this process with the opposite side of the design.

Combine the threads in the center. Use single outer strands from each side to tie three SQKTs around the rest of the threads. Thread a single bead on each strand and secure it with a coil knot. Repeat with the remaining strands. Trim each thread just below each coil knot as desired.

Macrame Gallery

Necklace knotted with nylon, sterling silver beads, and pearls. Elaine Lieberman

Waxed linen necklace with peacock pearls.
Elaine Lieberman

Choker knotted with coated copper wire, sterling silver cones, and freshwater pearls.
Elaine Lieberman

Pendant knotted with fine silver wire, Balinese and Turkish beads. Elaine Lieberman

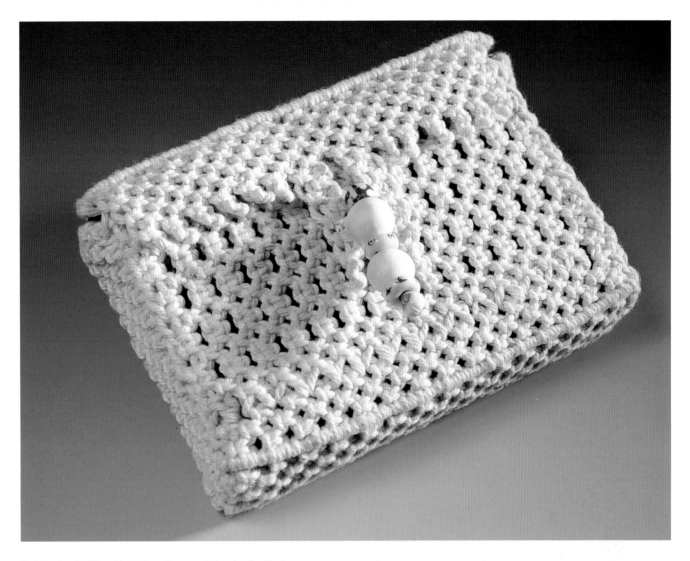

Belt bag knotted in cotton twine with ceramic beads. Jim Gentry

Linen chokers with
synthetic beads.
Jim Gentry

Necklace pouches knotted with cotton thread, glass, and ceramic beads.
Jim Gentry

Linen neckpiece with wood and metal beads.
Jim Gentry

Cotton thread wristbands. Jim Gentry

ACKNOWLEDGMENTS

Any endeavor is the culmination of one's life experiences—a result of the inspirations and influences which shape who we are. From this perspective I must express appreciation to my parents, who always supported me in my pursuit of education; my teachers, who let me know they believed in me; and my students, who made each day an adventure.

Lark Books is due countless thanks for all the years it brought richness to my life through *FIBERARTS* magazine and numerous craft publications. Thanks to Katie Dumont, editor of *THE NEW MACRAME* (Lark, 2000), who expressed enthusiasm for my work.

The staff at Lark has made the process of writing this book a pleasure. After observing Evan Bracken at work, I'll never view photographs in the same light! Susan McBride beautifully demonstrated what the art in art directing meant. Terry Taylor's knowledge and vision of how to get text, photographs, and illustrations together to serve the reader amazed me. (Those macrame lessons I gave you in 1972 finally paid off!) Thanks to you all, again.

Thanks are also due Carol Taylor, Deborah Morgenthal, and Rob Pulleyn, whose decision to publish this book has made a life-long dream a reality.

And speaking of dreams, here's one for the future: That my granddaughters Olivia, Amelia, and MaKenzie will find a spark in this book which inspires them to try knotting. Plenty of thread will be ready when you are!

INDEX

ELAINE LIEBERMAN creates jewelry, hangings, and other unique knotted pieces. She teaches classes in jewelry making and macrame. You can view more of her work online at www.elainecraft.com.